Grammar and Writing Skills Practice & Apply: Grades 7+

BY

BOB KERR

COPYRIGHT © 2000 Mark Twain Media, Inc.

ISBN   10-digit: 1-58037-126-4
         13-digit: 978-1-58037-126-1

Printing No. CD-1348

Mark Twain Media, Inc., Publishers
Distributed by Carson-Dellosa Publishing Company, Inc.

Table of Contents

Table of Contents

Table of Contents

Introduction

This practice book for grammar and writing covers most content areas. Beginning with parts of speech and concluding with creative writing, students reinforce skills through a variety of exercises and tests. The emphasis of this book is on the fundamentals of the English language. Students reinforce basic rules, work on exercises, and apply those skills through writing assignments.

Three features highlight this book. (1) Tests at the end of each unit are designed to help students practice the standardized testing format seldom used in the normal classroom situation. (2) All key grammatical terms in bold type appear in a glossary at the end of the book. (3) A writing application section supplies a writing prompt for each subject area. Students are challenged to write creatively and yet focus on basic grammatical skills.

Name: _____   Date: _____

Unit 1: *Kinds of Nouns*

Tip

A **proper noun** names a particular person, place, idea, or thing. **Proper nouns** begin with a capital letter. All other **nouns** are **common nouns**.

Practice

Directions: Underline all nouns in the following sentences. Circle any letters that should be capitalized.

1. Kayla, give that book to your teacher, please.
2. atlanta and detroit are cities I would like to visit.
3. washington, d.c., is the capital of the united states.
4. The team will play football in the new stadium on Friday.
5. In what year was abraham lincoln elected president?
6. The title of the book is silas marner.

Tip

A **concrete noun** names something that is felt with the senses. An **abstract noun** names a quality, idea, or state of mind.

Example:
The tourists at Disney World wait with anticipation.
(concrete)   (concrete)   (abstract)

Practice

Directions: Put the nouns on the left in the correct column below.

	Concrete Nouns	**Abstract Nouns**
wind		
joy	1. _____	1. _____
pride		
cotton	2. _____	2. _____
chocolate		
music	3. _____	3. _____
anger		
forgiveness	4. _____	4. _____

Name: _____   Date: _____

Unit 1: *Using Nouns*

Practice

Directions: Complete each sentence with an appropriate noun. Write what kind of noun it is on the line: **proper**, **concrete**, or **abstract**.

> **Example:** *John laughed when he heard the <u>story</u>.* <u>concrete</u>

1. Max gave the permission slip to his _____. _____

2. My family went to _____ for our vacation. _____

3. Lynn was full of _____ as she watched the movie. _____

4. My favorite food is _____. _____

5. _____ is my next-door neighbor. _____

6. Miguel's brother borrowed his _____ yesterday. _____

7. It takes _____ to compete in a decathlon. _____

8. Last night we played _____ at the party. _____

Tip

Form the plural of most **nouns** by adding "s." *car - cars*
To **nouns** ending with a vowel and "y," add "s." *toy - toys*
To **nouns** ending with a consonant and "y," change the "y" to "i" and add "es."
   spy - spies

Practice

Directions: Change the following phrases to plural nouns.

1. that boy   _____

2. any person   _____

3. a solo   _____

4. this culture   _____

Name: _____ Date: _____

Unit 1: *Possessive Nouns*

Tip

Form the possessive of a **plural noun** ending in **"s"** by adding only an apostrophe ('). For **singular** or **plural nouns** not ending in **"s,"** show possession by adding an apostrophe and an **"s."** ('**s**).

Examples:

Singular	*Anna's boots are new.*
Plural	*The men's clinic opened recently.*
Plural	*Lions' manes are often full and fluffy.*

Practice

Directions: Change these nouns to singular possessive, plural, and plural possessive.

Singular	Singular Possessive	Plural	Plural Possessive
1. army	_____	_____	_____
2. judge	_____	_____	_____
3. tooth	_____	_____	_____
4. story	_____	_____	_____
5. knife	_____	_____	_____

Directions: Choose the correct noun to complete the phrase and write the correct possessive form of it in the blank.

horse	**honey**	**secretary**	**alto**
house	**club**	**brush**	**teacher**

1. (plural) _____ sharp bristles

2. (singular) _____ beautiful voice

3. (singular) _____ sweet taste

4. (singular) _____ shiny coat

5. (plural) _____ new computers

6. (plural) _____ fresh paint

7. (singular) _____ favorite class

Name: _____ Date: _____

Unit 1: *Plural Nouns Crossword*

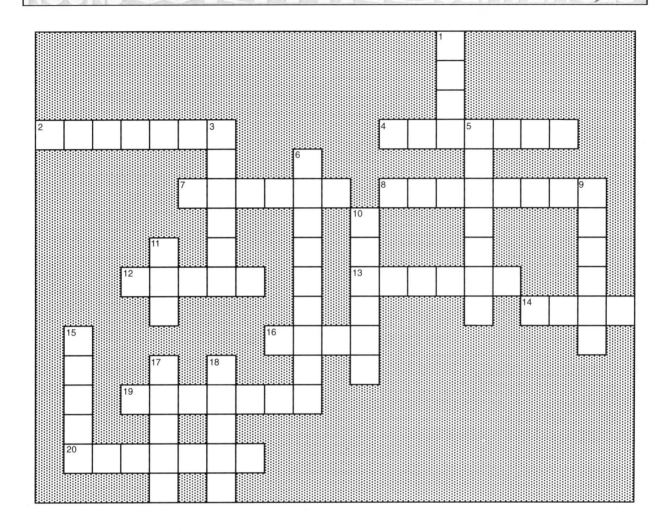

Directions: Write the plural of each noun listed below in the corresponding box in the puzzle.

ACROSS	DOWN
2. puppy	1. deer
4. porch	3. swamp
7. radio	5. class
8. potato	6. country
12. goose	9. self
13. leaf	10. half
14. ox	11. man
16. mouse	15. trout
19. monkey	17. fox
20. thief	18. sky

Name: _____ Date: _____

Unit 1: *Subject & Object Pronouns, Personal & Possessive Pronouns*

Practice

Directions: Read the descriptions below about each type of pronoun. Underline all the pronouns in each sentence. Then, under each description, find the pronouns of that type in the sentences and write them on the lines.

Personal pronouns take the place of one or more **nouns**.

1. We enjoyed the game last night.

2. Thanks for asking us to attend.

3. They played very well.

_____ _____ _____

Subject pronouns are used as the **subject** of a **sentence**.

1. She borrowed my jacket for the party.

2. We will be happy when our friends arrive.

3. I always like to dance with you.

_____ _____ _____

Object pronouns can be used as a **direct object**, **indirect object**, or an **object of a preposition**.

1. Mia showed me the photos from her vacation.

2. She told her friends that she bought souvenirs for them.

3. They were grateful and remembered to thank her.

_____ _____ _____

Possessive pronouns are personal **pronouns** that show possession or ownership.

1. Jackie introduced her father to the class.

2. He told us about the job as mayor of our town.

3. Jackie's father is busier than mine.

_____ _____ _____

Name: _____ Date: _____

Unit 1: *Other Types of Pronouns*

Tip

An **interrogative pronoun** introduces an interrogative sentence.

Examples: *Who owns the car?*
                Whom did you call?

(Note: Be careful to use "who" as the **subject** of a **sentence** and "whom" as the **object**.)

A **reflexive pronoun** reflects the action of the **verb** back to the **subject**.

Example: *I introduced myself to the new student.*

An **intensive pronoun** adds emphasis to a **noun** or **pronoun** just named.

Example: *The woman herself has not yet been told.*

An **indefinite pronoun** may refer to a **noun** but does not indicate a specific person, place, or thing.

Example: *Someone caught the foul ball.*

Practice

Directions: Underline the pronoun in each sentence and write what type of pronoun it is.

1. Most of the people heard the alarm. _____
2. Napoleon declared himself the emperor of France. _____
3. What is the answer to question three? _____
4. Anyone can obtain a library card. _____
5. The players themselves don't know the score. _____
6. Which of the puppies belongs to Sierra? _____
7. Deborah bought herself a snack in the cafeteria. _____
8. The canyon itself has never been explored. _____

Writing Application

Directions: Write three sentences of your own on your own paper. Use at least one pronoun in each sentence.

Name: _____ Date: _____

Unit 1: *Using Pronouns*

Practice

Directions: Complete each sentence by adding an appropriate interrogative, reflexive, intensive, possessive, or indefinite pronoun. Write what kind of pronoun you used on the line beside the sentence.

1. Jacob let Sarah play with _____ ball. _____

2. _____ of the cakes did you bring? _____

3. Brevin pulled _____ onto the platform. _____

4. Madison told _____ to be here at 3:00. _____

5. _____ was voted class president this year? _____

6. _____ of the questions can be left blank. _____

Writing Application

1. Write a sentence using "himself" as a **reflexive pronoun**.

   _____

2. Write a sentence using "anyone" as an **indefinite pronoun**.

   _____

3. Write a sentence using "which" as an **interrogative pronoun**.

   _____

4. Write a sentence using "you" as an **object pronoun**.

   _____

5. Write a sentence using "our" as a **possessive pronoun**.

   _____

6. Write a sentence using "they" as a **subject pronoun**.

   _____

Name: _____ Date: _____

Unit 1: *Adjectives/Demonstrative Adjectives*

Tip

An **adjective** describes a **noun** or **pronoun**. **Adjectives** usually come just before the **noun** or **pronoun**.

Practice

Directions: Underline all the adjectives in the sentences below.

1. Large groups of people camp at this beautiful lake over the long weekend.

2. Excited children rush to the sandy beach for a cool swim.

3. Two men are playing catch under the shady elm tree.

4. Interested observers watch the noisy speedboats rush by.

5. Many boats have daring skiers behind them, skidding across the rough waves.

6. Three peaceful fishermen sit in an anchored boat on the far side of the lake.

Tip

"This," "that," "these," and "those" are **demonstrative adjectives** that modify **nouns** by telling **which one** or **which ones**.

    Examples: *This car is a convertible.*
                        That car across the street is a hatchback.

Practice

Directions: Circle the correct form of the adjective in parentheses.

1. (This, That) man over there is very tall.

2. (Those, That) shoes look too big for you.

3. (These, This) pair might be better.

4. (That, Those) dog looks vicious.

Name: _____   Date: _____

Unit 1: *Comparing With Adjectives*

Tip

Adjectives can be used to compare two or more **nouns**. The word endings "er" or "est" or special words such as "less," "least," "more," and "most" are added to show comparison.

Examples:

	Comparative	Superlative
angry	*angrier*	*angriest*
fun	*less fun*	*least fun*

Practice

Directions: Write a comparative and superlative form of each adjective.

		Comparative	**Superlative**
1.	daring	_____	_____
2.	skinny	_____	_____
3.	active	_____	_____
4.	small	_____	_____
5.	easy	_____	_____
6.	slow	_____	_____
7.	quiet	_____	_____
8.	dark	_____	_____

Directions: Write the correct form of the adjective in parentheses. (Note: these are adjectives that have irregular comparison forms.)

1. Now that his arm has healed, Bo is feeling _____. (good)

2. I have _____ cats, but Julie has _____ of them. (many)

3. My answer is _____, but it could be _____. (bad)

4. They saved the _____ for last. (good)

5. I have _____ money now than I did yesterday. (little)

Name: _____   Date: _____

Unit 1: *Comparing With Adjectives*

Practice

Directions: Fill in each blank with an adjective that makes sense in the sentence.

1. Lenny is _____ than his younger brother Brian.

2. The _____ group has five members.

3. Your goldfish looks _____ in his tank.

4. I performed _____ on the test than the other students.

5. At the store, a _____ cashier took my coupon.

6. As the other team scored a goal, I grew _____.

7. You have a very _____ and _____ mother.

8. I have always liked _____ movies.

Directions: To make your writing detailed and descriptive, practice using adjectives. For each noun, supply one or more appropriate adjectives.

Example:
    group   *rowdy group*

1. party   _____

2. quarterback _____

3. house   _____

4. truck   _____

5. day   _____

6. hamster   _____

Writing Application

Directions: Write a paragraph on your own paper describing your best friend. Use as many adjectives as you can and then underline them when you finish.

11

Name: _____ Date: _____

Unit 1: *Pronoun or Adjective?*

Practice

Directions: On the blank line write **Pronoun** if the underlined word is used as a pronoun, or **Adjective** if it is used as an adjective.

Example: *Most players prefer playing on turf.*   Adjective

1. Few enjoy the symphony like I do. _____

2. Did you bring a snack for both children? _____

3. Someone returned the missing videotape. _____

4. Both of the students passed the spelling test. _____

5. All visitors are welcome at the center. _____

6. Several of them got lost on the way to the party. _____

7. This will soon be over. _____

Directions: Use the words below as either pronouns or adjectives in sentences of your own.

1. ("all" as a pronoun)

   _____

2. ("many" as an adjective)

   _____

3. ("this" as an adjective)

   _____

4. ("someone" as a pronoun)

   _____

5. ("every" as an adjective)

   _____

Name: _____   Date: _____

Unit 1: *Principal Parts of Verbs*

Tip

Every **verb** has four principal parts: the **present**, the **present participle**, the **past**, and the **past participle**.

Present	Present Participle	Past	Past Participle
look	looking	looked	(have) looked

Tip

Most **verbs** are regular and form their **past** and **past participles** by adding "d" or "ed." But some **verbs** are irregular and form their **past** and **past participles** differently.

Present	Present Participle	Past	Past Participle
begin	beginning	began	(have) begun
buy	buying	bought	(have) bought
forget	forgetting	forgot	(have) forgotten
grow	growing	grew	(have) grown
set	setting	set	(have) set

Practice

Directions: See how many of the following irregular verbs you already know. Complete the last three principal parts.

Present	Present Participle	Past	Past Participle
1. sit	_____	_____	_____
2. bite	_____	_____	_____
3. lie	_____	_____	_____
4. go	_____	_____	_____
5. burst	_____	_____	_____
6. ring	_____	_____	_____
7. sing	_____	_____	_____
8. lose	_____	_____	_____
9. blow	_____	_____	_____
10. raise	_____	_____	_____
11. steal	_____	_____	_____

Name: _____   Date: _____

Unit 1: *Using the Principal Parts of Verbs*

Practice

Directions: For each sentence, write the correct form—past or past participle—for the verbs in parentheses.

1. They _____ a new captain last year. (choose)

2. Have you ever _____ in a plane? (ride)

3. Many of the guests had _____ by that time. (go)

4. I have _____ Mom's favorite cup. (broke)

5. Has he _____ his assignment? (forget)

6. By Thursday, my report will have been _____. (write)

7. Manny hasn't even _____ to write his. (begin)

8. The letter hasn't _____ yet. (come)

9. John has _____ three inches. (grow)

10. I hadn't _____ it when you asked me. (see)

11. The teacher has _____ to my parents. (speak)

12. Henry _____ his work well this year. (do)

13. Prizes will be _____ before the party. (hide)

14. The faculty has already _____ lunch. (eat)

15. That lesson has _____ me all day. (take)

16. I didn't know that dog had _____ you. (bite)

Name: _____   Date: _____

Unit 1: *Action and State of Being Verbs*

Tip

A **verb** is a word that expresses action or state of being.

Practice

Directions: Circle the words that can be verbs.

was	elephant	believe	ridden	job	work
best	grab	large	looks	is	because

Directions: In the following sentences, underline action verbs and circle state of being verbs.

Example:

The early colonists were discontent.

1. After the French and Indian War, the colonists seemed happy.

2. They belonged to the British Empire.

3. The British government tried to enforce the Acts of Trade.

4. The Stamp Act passed, but later was rejected.

5. The Boston Tea Party was an open defiance.

Writing Application

Directions: Use the verbs you circled in the first exercise in original sentences on your own paper.

Name: _____   Date: _____

Unit 1: *Linking Verbs*

Tip

       A **linking verb** joins the **subject** to a **noun** or **adjective** in the **predicate**. Most **linking verbs** will be forms of the **verb** "be," but the other **linking verbs** are "taste," "feel," "smell," "look," "sound," "seem," "become," "appear," "remain," and "grow." You can tell if these **verbs** are *linking* by simply substituting the corresponding form of "be."

Example:

        This cloth <u>feels</u> smooth.
        This cloth <u>is</u> smooth.

Practice

Directions: If the verb is action, underline it. If it is linking, circle it.

1. Donald lifted the suitcase onto the bed.

2. The corn grew tall during August.

3. That was he whom you saw.

4. Joan handed the letter to Angie.

5. Who is the president of the French Club?

6. She seems to be sad today.

7. The dog smelled the food in its dish.

8. I will remain in the house.

Writing Application

Directions: Write original **sentences** on your own paper using "taste," "feel," "smell," "sound," and "appear" as **action** and as **linking verbs**. You will write ten total **sentences**.

     16

Name: _____ Date: _____

Unit 1: *Subject-Verb Agreement*

Tip

A **verb** must agree with its **subject** in person and number.

Examples: *John is here.*
              They are here.
              When were you going, Tom?
              The bouquet of roses is on the table.
              Irene and Jane are sisters.
              Either Bill or Steve was captain.

Practice

Directions: Circle the correct verb from the pair in parentheses.

Example: *Mathematics (is, are) my favorite subject.*

1. A crate of oranges (was, were) loaded on the truck.

2. Where (was, were) you when I called?

3. There (is, are) only one shoe here.

4. Athletics (require, requires) attention to good health.

5. Ralph and Paul (doesn't, don't) have to go in yet.

6. (Is, Are) Bill and Steve in Boy Scouts?

7. Stacey and Annette (is, are) going to the game tonight.

8. Skiing and skating (is, are) my favorite winter sports.

9. Why (is, are) he your choice of partners?

10. The bathroom scales (needs, need) replacing.

Writing Application

Directions: Write a paragraph on your own paper on what you feel about TV violence. Check your subject-verb agreement.

17

Name: _____   Date: _____

Unit 1: *Reviewing Verbs*

Practice

Directions: Underline the verb or verb phrase in each sentence.

1. The plans have been made for the hike on Monday.

2. The lake was completely frozen by noon.

3. The children came quietly from the gymnasium.

4. Have you read many books this summer?

5. John will develop the negative.

6. Rhonda could not understand the assignment.

7. We will be questioned by the teacher today.

8. Mrs. Service has already spoken to my parents.

9. Those vegetables were raised in Alabama.

10. The money will be collected Monday morning.

11. The bell has been ringing.

12. The waitress will bring our orders very soon.

13. Do not take the chairs from the room.

14. In the afternoon, the temperature rose slowly.

15. Who opened the door for us?

16. Swimming classes have been rescheduled for this week.

17. I have attended this school since third grade.

18. The flower appears very tiny in that large vase.

Name: _____   Date: _____

Unit 1: *Adverbs*

Tip

Adverbs modify **verbs, adjectives,** or other **adverbs**. Adverbs are used to answer the questions "how," "when," " where," "how often," "how much," and "to what extent."

Examples: *Eric will arrive <u>later</u>. (answers "when")*
Dad drives <u>slowly</u>. (answers "how")

Note: **adverbs** that modify **adverbs** are called "qualifiers" or "intensifiers."

Example: *She walks <u>quite</u> fast.*

Practice

Directions: In these phrases underline the adverb and circle the word it modifies. On the first line, tell what question the adverb answers. On the second line, tell what part of speech the adverb modifies.

	Question Answered	Part of Speech Modified
1. she dances gracefully	_____	_____
2. is leaving now	_____	_____
3. always calls home	_____	_____
4. was thrown out	_____	_____
5. is fully prepared	_____	_____

Tip

Many **adverbs** can be formed by adding "ly" or "ily" to an **adjective**.

Examples: *brief - briefly   ordinary - ordinarily*

Practice

Directions: Make adverbs from these adjectives by adding the correct ending.

1. terrible _____
2. heavy _____
3. usual _____
4. vague _____
5. soft _____
6. important _____

Name: _____   Date: _____

Unit 1: *Using Adverbs*

Practice

Directions: Fill in the blank with an appropriate adverb.

1. Mack jogged _____ down the path.

2. I went to the fair _____.

3. Always play the game _____.

4. The boxes fell _____ the stairs.

5. Hannah practiced her flute at my house _____.

Directions: For each adverb, write a sentence of your own using the adverb appropriately.

1. (later) _____

   _____

2. (outside) _____

   _____

3. (totally) _____

   _____

4. (well) _____

   _____

5. (carefully) _____

   _____

6. (recently) _____

   _____

7. (quickly) _____

   _____

Name: _____ Date: _____

Unit 1: *Adjectives and Adverbs*

Tip

Adverbs generally answer "how," "when," "where," "how often," "how much," and "to what extent." **Adjectives** answer "what kind," "which one," and "how many."

Practice

Directions: Cross out the word that is not correct. Write **Adj.** or **Adv.** above the correct word.

1. This form must be completed (accurate, accurately).

2. Your shirt looks (sloppy, sloppily).

3. You can dress (sloppy, sloppily) on the weekend.

4. The kittens were (warm, warmly) under the blanket.

5. Tina plays softball (skillful, skillfully).

6. The train ride to San Francisco was (slow, slowly).

7. The horse plodded (heavy, heavily) down the trail.

8. My street is (smooth, smoothly) enough for skateboarding.

Directions: Circle the adjectives and underline the adverbs.

1. The lively puppy trotted quickly to the door.

2. When the little boy opened the door, the puppy ran outside.

3. Two chattering birds flew dangerously close to the dog's head.

4. The playful puppy barked loudly at the birds as they flew away.

5. Then he grew tired and came inside to rest.

6. The sleepy puppy was soon curled cozily in front of the warm fireplace.

     21

Name: _____ Date: _____

Unit 1: *Modifiers*

Practice

Directions: Label the underlined modifiers in each sentence. Write "A" over adjectives, "NM" over noun modifiers (nouns used as adjectives) and "VM" over verb modifiers (verbs used as adjectives).

      Example: *A   NM*
                    Our favorite family doctor moved away.

1. The large, sliding avalanche was a danger to skiers.

2. He painted a sad, drooping face on the clown.

3. The drizzling rain ruined our cardboard clubhouse.

4. The generous church donation allowed the group to visit Central America.

5. The successful running back set our school record.

6. My hospital bill was costly.

7. The purple blooming flowers attracted bumble bees.

8. The plastic and glass necklace looked real.

9. The blaring fire alarm startled everyone.

10. A green swimming turtle moved smoothly through the water.

Name: _____ Date: _____

Unit 1: *Direct Objects*

Tip

A **direct object** is a word that tells who or what receives the action of the **verb**.
Example:
> Annette adjusted the <u>volume</u> on the radio. *(answers "what")*

In some **sentences**, the **direct object** is compound.
Example:
> Grandmother gave <u>money</u> and <u>clothes</u> to the charity. *(answers "what")*

Practice

Directions: Underline the verb and circle the direct object in each sentence.

1. Mimi called Mr. Robbins last night.

2. The actor memorized his lines for the play.

3. The nurse checked my pulse.

4. The club elected Scott as treasurer.

5. James wrote a poem for English homework.

6. Sharon lost her best earrings.

7. Many people read the newspaper daily.

8. The store lost business after the fire.

9. I invited Manny to the dance.

10. That photographer takes beautiful pictures.

11. Melinda visited China last year.

12. Brandi collects foreign stamps.

13. I make my bed every morning.

14. I wore Jen's dress to the dance.

15. Ben asked me to join his team.

Name: _____   Date: _____

Unit 1: *Using Direct Objects*

Practice

Directions: Complete the following sentences by supplying an appropriate direct object.

> **Example:** *Leah owns <u>horses</u>.*

1. Vince likes _____.

2. The committee elected _____.

3. Glen plays _____.

4. My father chose _____.

5. She watched _____.

6. Ryan saw _____.

7. I ordered _____.

8. Alana helped _____.

9. They remembered _____.

10. The dog ate _____.

Writing Application

Directions: Write a paragraph on your own paper about what you do in the afternoons after school. Describe your activities and use direct objects in some of your sentences.

Name: _____　　Date: _____

Unit 1: *Indirect Objects*

Tip

An **indirect object** is a noun or pronoun that tells "to whom" or "for whom" the action of the **verb** is done.

　　Example:　　*Ms. Nelson told <u>us</u> a funny story.*
　　　　　　　　　　　 S 　　　V 　I.O.　　　D.O.

Practice

Directions: Label the subject (S), verb (V), direct object (D.O.), and indirect object (I.O.) in each sentence.

　　Example:　　　　　 S 　　 V 　 I.O.　　 D.O.
　　　　　　　　　　The teacher handed Joe his assignment.

1.　The bird provides her babies worms to eat.

2.　My uncle taught me fishing techniques.

3.　The group made their sponsor thank-you cards.

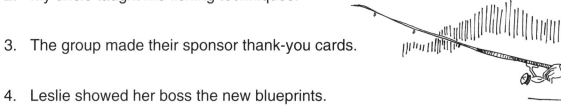

4.　Leslie showed her boss the new blueprints.

5.　The reporter read us his latest column.

6.　Our teacher left the substitute the answer key.

7.　The scientist gave the world a cure for the disease.

8.　Someone showed me the right road to take.

9.　You sent Nate a long e-mail.

10.　Simon told her the correct address.

　　　　25

Name: _____   Date: _____

Unit 1: *Using Indirect Objects*

Practice

Directions: Complete each sentence with an indirect object.

1. Mr. Brown offered _____ two tickets to the concert.

2. Grandma made _____ a meatloaf tonight.

3. I sent _____ a belated birthday card.

4. Coach Stewart promised _____ the starting position.

5. Mr. Hardman teaches _____ Mandarin Chinese.

6. The president presented _____ the medal of honor.

7. She told _____ all the answers.

8. Dion promised _____ the last cookie.

9. They gave _____ first choice.

10. The boss showed _____ the cash register codes.

Writing Application

Directions: Write five sentences of your own that contain indirect objects. After you have written them, label the subject, verb, direct object, and indirect object.

   Example: *S   V   I.O.   D.O.*
                    She handed Lori the microphone.

_____

_____

_____

_____

_____

Name: _____ Date: _____

Unit 1: *Conjunctions*

Tip

A **coordinating conjunction** is used to connect two ideas of relatively equal importance.

> **Example:**   *Did they take a boat or a plane?*

Coordinating Conjunctions

and	but	or
for	nor	yet

A **subordinating conjunction** is used to show the connection between a **dependent clause** and the rest of the **sentence**.

> **Example:**   *We will leave when Sam arrives.*

Subordinating Conjunctions

if	until	although
as	when	because
since	unless	before

A **correlative conjunction** is used to show contrast between two ideas.

> **Example:**   *The tree is either a maple or an oak.*

Correlative Conjunctions

not only. . . but also	either. . . or
whether. . . if	neither. . . nor

Practice

Directions: Underline the conjunction in each sentence. On the line write **coordinating**, **subordinating**, or **correlative** to indicate how the conjunction is used.

1. Neither Alan nor I had done our homework. _____

2. The picnic will be tomorrow unless it rains. _____

3. In the summer I like to fish and swim. _____

4. John will lose the race unless he hurries. _____

5. They invited us, but we forgot to attend. _____

6. Trish won the award, for she had worked the hardest. _____

Name: _____   Date: _____

Unit 1: *Using Conjunctions*

Practice

Directions: Write an appropriate conjunction to complete each sentence.

1. Dad got promoted _____ he did that extra project.

2. Haven't you either visited Gary _____ called him?

3. It may sound funny, _____ the album is very good.

4. Dolphins not only communicate, _____ learn.

5. Your horse can go over the bridge _____ walk through the creek.

6. _____ it snows, the trip will be canceled.

7. The freshman class _____ the junior high built the float together.

8. I can't come over _____ an adult is present.

Directions: Combine the sentences below using a subordinating conjunction from the box. Use a different subordinating conjunction each time.

because	if	after
whenever	until	before

1. We plan to ride our bikes. It rains.

   _____

2. You can stay home. You are concerned about lightning.

   _____

3. Maybe we should all wait. The rain stops.

   _____

4. Chances for an accident increase. The road is slippery.

   _____

5. I must remember to wear my helmet. I have fallen before.

   _____

Name: _____ Date: _____

Unit 1: *Prepositions*

Tip

A **preposition** shows a relationship between a **noun** or **pronoun** (the **object**) and another word in the **sentence.**

Example: *prep.*   *obj.*
               He threw the ball <u>through</u> the goal.

Practice

Directions: Write an object for each preposition.

1. upon _____
2. beneath _____
3. from _____
4. in _____
5. above _____
6. under _____
7. to _____
8. near _____
9. beside _____
10. on _____

Directions: Circle the preposition in each sentence and underline the object of the preposition.

Example: *I dropped my keys ⟨into⟩ my <u>purse</u>.*

1. On a summer day, people like to be outdoors.

2. A young girl swam toward the dock.

3. A wasp flew into the house.

4. Smoke from the grill filled the air.

5. The fisherman leaned against a rock while fishing.

6. Angel's flowered kite blew in the wind.

7. After school, the Johnson kids headed to the park.

8. Little children were climbing on the jungle gym.

9. Steve jumped off the diving board.

10. A squirrel scrambled up the nearest tree.

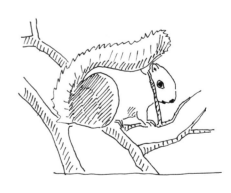

Name: _____ Date: _____

Unit 1: *Prepositional Phrases*

Tip

A **prepositional phrase** is a group of words that begins with a **preposition** and ends with a **noun** or **pronoun**.

Example: *Chicago is located near the lake.*

Practice

Directions: Underline the prepositional phrases in each sentence. Circle the objects of prepositions. The first one is done for you.

1. Corey went to the movie with Sara.

2. My cat drinks water from the kitchen sink.

3. The plane soared from the runway into the sky.

4. The school bus slowed to a halt at the railroad crossing.

Directions: Use each preposition in a sentence of your own. Put parentheses around the prepositional phrase.

1. above _____

2. up _____

3. against _____

4. on _____

5. beside _____

6. from _____

7. near _____

8. at _____

Name: _____ Date: _____

Unit 1: *Prepositional Phrases as Adjectives and Adverbs*

Tip

When a **prepositional phrase** modifies a **noun**, it acts as an **adjective**.

Example: *The street to the right leads home.*
                    (phrase modifies "street")

When a **prepositional phrase** modifies a **verb**, it acts as an **adverb**.

Example: *Today Martha left for the airport.*
                    (phrase modifies "left")

Practice

Directions: On the line after each sentence, write **ADJ** if the prepositional phrase functions as an adjective in the sentence, and write **ADV** if the prepositional phrase functions as an adverb.

1. My family went to the circus. _____

2. The tent was pitched in a large field. _____

3. I liked the tiger with the black stripes. _____

4. One brave man balanced himself on the high wire. _____

5. The lady on horseback had grace and talent. _____

6. Several clowns climbed into a tiny car. _____

7. The people beside the lion cage heard the roars. _____

8. Near the end the crowd gave the circus loud applause. _____

Writing Application

Directions: Write five more sentences on your own paper describing what you might see, hear, or do at a circus. Use at least one prepositional phrase in each sentence.

31

Name: _____   Date: _____

Unit 1: *Finding and Using Prepositional Phrases*

Practice

Directions: Underline all the prepositional phrases in each sentence.

1. In a monarchy, the head of the country is a king or queen.

2. A democracy is any form of government that is elected by popular vote.

3. A nation with a dictator cannot have free elections.

4. Governments can make trade agreements with other countries.

5. The United Nations, an organization of many countries, meets in New York.

6. The United States of America has been an independent nation since 1776.

7. Across the ocean, Great Britain represents a long tradition of monarchy.

Writing Application

Directions: Pretend that you have gathered a group of people and pets for a photograph. Write five sentences describing how everyone should be positioned. Using the prepositions below, put a prepositional phrase in each sentence.

beside   near   onto   from   behind

_____

_____

_____

_____

_____

_____

_____

_____

_____

_____

Name: _____ Date: _____

Unit 1 Test 1: *Nouns*

Directions: Darken the circle under the word that is a possessive, proper, concrete, or abstract noun.

Example: *Which word is a proper noun?*

The team plays baseball in Atlanta.
  Ⓐ   Ⓑ   Ⓒ   **Ⓓ**

(D - "Atlanta" is a proper noun.)

1. *Which word is an abstract noun?*

   The leader told his group to have no fear.
     Ⓐ   Ⓑ   Ⓒ   Ⓓ

2. *Which word is a possessive noun?*

   The turtle's shell has green and brown spots.
     Ⓐ   Ⓑ   Ⓒ   Ⓓ

3. *Which word is a concrete noun?*

   Seth told a story about love and forgiveness.
     Ⓐ   Ⓑ   Ⓒ   Ⓓ

4. *Which word is a proper noun?*

   Mr. Reynolds gave the kids a ride in his new truck.
       Ⓐ   Ⓑ   Ⓒ   Ⓓ

5. *Which word is an abstract noun?*

   They say envy is a green-eyed monster.
     Ⓐ   Ⓑ   Ⓒ   Ⓓ

6. *Which word is a possessive noun?*

   The trainer rubbed oils on the quarterback's arm.
     Ⓐ   Ⓑ   Ⓒ   Ⓓ

7. *Which word is a concrete noun?*

   At the ceremony Janet felt great pride.
        Ⓐ   Ⓑ Ⓒ Ⓓ

8. *Which word is a proper noun?*

   My cousin visited Rome during his vacation.
      Ⓐ   Ⓑ Ⓒ   Ⓓ

Name: _____   Date: _____

Unit 1 Test 2: *Pronouns*

Directions: Darken the letter beside the correct pronoun.

Example: *We enjoyed* _____ *performance tonight.*
Ⓐ hers   Ⓑ she   Ⓒ her   Ⓓ them
(C - "her" is the correct possessive pronoun)

1. It was _____ who bought the soda.
    Ⓐ she   Ⓑ her   Ⓒ hers   Ⓓ him

2. Please tell _____ that I borrowed his watch.
    Ⓐ they   Ⓑ its   Ⓒ he   Ⓓ him

3. Marcy showed _____ her favorite movie.
    Ⓐ me   Ⓑ I   Ⓒ she   Ⓓ hers

4. Carmela and _____ did the project together.
    Ⓐ him   Ⓑ me   Ⓒ he   Ⓓ them

Directions: Darken the letter beside the word that describes the function of the underlined pronoun.

Example: *She bought* <u>herself</u> *a new coat.*
Ⓐ reflexive   Ⓑ possessive   Ⓒ intensive   Ⓓ interrogative
(A - "herself" functions as a reflexive pronoun)

1. Did he invite <u>someone</u> to the dance?
    Ⓐ interrogative   Ⓑ reflexive   Ⓒ possessive   Ⓓ indefinite

2. The volcano <u>itself</u> has never done any damage.
    Ⓐ interrogative   Ⓑ reflexive   Ⓒ intensive   Ⓓ indefinite

3. The horse shook off <u>its</u> reins.
    Ⓐ interrogative   Ⓑ reflexive   Ⓒ intensive   Ⓓ possessive

34

Name: _____   Date: _____

Unit 1 Test 3: *Adjectives and Adverbs*

Directions: Darken the circle under the word that is an adverb or adjective. Darken "E" if the correct answer is not given.

Example: *Which word is an adverb?*

Dad <u>slowly</u> <u>opened</u> the <u>heavy</u> <u>chest</u>.
     Ⓐ   Ⓑ   Ⓒ   Ⓓ   Ⓔ *not given*

(A – "slowly" modifies the verb "opened")

1. *Which word is an adverb?*

   <u>Brandy</u> put her <u>excited</u> <u>puppy</u> <u>outside</u>.
     Ⓐ   Ⓑ   Ⓒ   Ⓓ   Ⓔ not given

2. *Which word is an adjective?*

   <u>Those</u> bananas have been <u>there</u> <u>since</u> <u>Saturday</u>.
     Ⓐ   Ⓑ   Ⓒ   Ⓓ   Ⓔ not given

3. *Which word is an adverb?*

   Dan is <u>quickly</u> <u>becoming</u> the <u>tallest</u> <u>student</u> in class.
        Ⓐ   Ⓑ   Ⓒ   Ⓓ   Ⓔ not given

4. *Which word is an adjective?*

   <u>Five</u> <u>birds</u> chirped <u>loudly</u> all <u>morning</u>.
     Ⓐ   Ⓑ   Ⓒ   Ⓓ   Ⓔ not given

5. *Which word is an adverb?*

   <u>Several</u> <u>people</u> visited the <u>new</u> museum <u>this</u> week.
     Ⓐ   Ⓑ   Ⓒ   Ⓓ   Ⓔ not given

6. *Which word is an adjective?*

   North Carolina <u>has</u> some of the <u>prettiest</u> <u>scenery</u> in the <u>nation</u>.
           Ⓐ   Ⓑ   Ⓒ   Ⓓ   Ⓔ not given

7. *Which word is an adverb?*

   The <u>document</u> is <u>accurate</u> and has been <u>carefully</u> <u>copied</u>.
       Ⓐ   Ⓑ   Ⓒ   Ⓓ   Ⓔ not given

8. *Which word is an adjective?*

   A <u>large</u> <u>elephant</u> lumbered <u>slowly</u> <u>toward</u> the zookeeper.
      Ⓐ   Ⓑ   Ⓒ   Ⓓ   Ⓔ not given

Name: _____   Date: _____

Unit 1 Test 4: *Verbs*

Directions: Darken the circle under the word that correctly tells the use of the underlined verb.

Example: *They <u>built</u> a fortress on that site.*
Ⓐ *linking*   Ⓑ *helping*   ● *action*

1. Did he <u>have</u> binoculars?
   Ⓐ linking   Ⓑ helping   Ⓒ action

2. Plans have been <u>made</u> for the hike.
   Ⓐ linking   Ⓑ helping   Ⓒ action

3. We <u>could</u> see the sunset from our window.
   Ⓐ linking   Ⓑ helping   Ⓒ action

4. I <u>will</u> meet you at the drugstore.
   Ⓐ linking   Ⓑ helping   Ⓒ action

5. My sister has <u>worked</u> hard this year.
   Ⓐ linking   Ⓑ helping   Ⓒ action

6. Diane <u>seemed</u> angry today.
   Ⓐ linking   Ⓑ helping   Ⓒ action

7. John will <u>develop</u> the negative.
   Ⓐ linking   Ⓑ helping   Ⓒ action

8. <u>Have</u> you read many books this year?
   Ⓐ linking   Ⓑ helping   Ⓒ action

9. Jessie <u>appears</u> tired since the game.
   Ⓐ linking   Ⓑ helping   Ⓒ action

10. My aunt <u>will</u> visit me again this summer.
    Ⓐ linking   Ⓑ helping   Ⓒ action

11. Who <u>opened</u> the door for us?
    Ⓐ linking   Ⓑ helping   Ⓒ action

12. The cashier <u>was</u> completely surprised by the sirens.
    Ⓐ linking   Ⓑ helping   Ⓒ action

Name: _____   Date: _____

Unit 1 Test 5: *Direct and Indirect Objects*

Directions: Darken the circle to show whether the underlined word functions as a direct or indirect object.

1. Keith gave <u>me</u> a CD for Christmas.
   - (A) direct
   - (B) indirect

2. The neighbor's dog buried her <u>bone</u> in our yard.
   - (A) direct
   - (B) indirect

3. June and Mason forgot to tell <u>you</u> the news.
   - (A) direct
   - (B) indirect

4. The cashier handed <u>me</u> the change.
   - (A) direct
   - (B) indirect

5. Grandma mailed <u>us</u> a thank-you card.
   - (A) direct
   - (B) indirect

Directions: Darken the circle beside the line that contains a direct or indirect object. Darken "D" if there is no correct answer.

1. *Which line contains a direct object?*
   - (A) Someone called and
   - (B) gave Aunt Leigh
   - (C) your new address.
   - (D) none

2. *Which line contains an indirect object?*
   - (A) My bicycle is broken. If I cannot
   - (B) fix the chain, will you loan me
   - (C) your old bike for the week?
   - (D) none

3. *Which line contains an indirect object?*
   - (A) I hear that Devin
   - (B) and his brother got a pet snake
   - (C) for Christmas. I hope I never see it!
   - (D) none

Name: _____ Date: _____

Unit 1 Test 6: *Conjunctions*

Directions: Darken the circle beside the **conjunction** that best completes the sentence.

     Example: *I will only go _____ you will come with me.*
            Ⓐ *but*   ⬤Ⓑ *if*   Ⓒ *nor*   Ⓓ *as*

1. Kate raked the leaves _____ her mother bagged them.
   Ⓐ and   Ⓑ or   Ⓒ although   Ⓓ unless

2. I have been excited _____ I heard the good news.
   Ⓐ yet   Ⓑ as   Ⓒ or   Ⓓ since

3. Sue _____ I will take the films back to the library.
   Ⓐ but   Ⓑ for   Ⓒ or   Ⓓ nor

4. I always buy popcorn _____ the movie starts.
   Ⓐ yet   Ⓑ before   Ⓒ or   Ⓓ but

5. I ordered the shrimp _____ I had never eaten it.
   Ⓐ before   Ⓑ nor   Ⓒ although   Ⓓ if

6. Isaiah wanted a dog _____ got a bird instead.
   Ⓐ but   Ⓑ since   Ⓒ because   Ⓓ for

7. He erased the chalkboard _____ the teacher asked him.
   Ⓐ nor   Ⓑ because   Ⓒ but   Ⓓ and

8. I will deliver the package, _____ you are available.
   Ⓐ and   Ⓑ or   Ⓒ when   Ⓓ nor

9. _____ Randall nor Bob has been at school today.
   Ⓐ or   Ⓑ neither   Ⓒ either   Ⓓ but

10. Can you help Lucy _____ Fran carry the boxes?
   Ⓐ after   Ⓑ because   Ⓒ and   Ⓓ nor

Name: _____ Date: _____

Unit 1 Test 7: *Prepositions*

Directions: Darken the circle beside the line that contains a prepositional phrase. Darken "D" if there is none.

Example:
   Ⓐ *I stood under the tree*
   Ⓑ *while my brother and*
   Ⓒ *Josh played catch.*
   Ⓓ *none*
   (A - "under the tree")

1. Ⓐ She borrowed a
   Ⓑ jacket from me
   Ⓒ because it was chilly.
   Ⓓ none

2. Ⓐ The silly jokes she
   Ⓑ told did not even
   Ⓒ make sense to me.
   Ⓓ none

3. Ⓐ Did you notice that Jesse
   Ⓑ has become very friendly since
   Ⓒ he decided to run for treasurer?
   Ⓓ none

4. Ⓐ From my point of view,
   Ⓑ it looks like the
   Ⓒ tower is leaning.
   Ⓓ none

5. Ⓐ Someone called you,
   Ⓑ but they did not leave
   Ⓒ a name or phone number.
   Ⓓ none

6. Ⓐ Research shows that most
   Ⓑ serious accidents occur
   Ⓒ in a person's own home.
   Ⓓ none

7. Ⓐ Standing behind the curtain,
   Ⓑ Rachel waited nervously
   Ⓒ because the crowd was so large.
   Ⓓ none

8. Ⓐ Becky has the tickets,
   Ⓑ but she is already headed
   Ⓒ toward the stadium.
   Ⓓ none

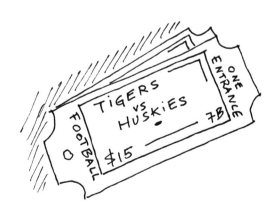

Name: _____ Date: _____

Unit 2: *Complete Subjects and Predicates*

Tip

The **subject** tells whom or what the **sentence** is about. All the words in the **subject** make up the **complete subject**.

Example: *The pilots on the plane gave the signal.*

The **predicate** tells what the **subject** is or does. All the words in the **predicate** make up the **complete predicate**.

Example: *Several cars pulled into the lot.*

Practice

Directions: Draw a slash between the complete subject and complete predicate.

1. Charles Dickens was a nineteenth-century writer.

2. He lived in England.

3. One of his most famous books is A Christmas Carol.

4. Ebenezer Scrooge and Tiny Tim both appear in the novel.

5. Tiny Tim's father, Bob, works for Scrooge.

6. Bob and his family are quite poor.

7. Three ghosts appear to Ebenezer one night.

8. One of them shows him how his life might end.

9. Scrooge decides to get into the Christmas spirit.

10. Dickens's book has become a part of our Christmas heritage.

Writing Application

Directions: In five or more sentences, retell a story or book, on your own paper, that you have read. In each sentence, draw a line between the complete subject and complete predicate.

Name: _____   Date: _____

Unit 2: *Writing Complete Subjects and Predicates*

Practice

Directions: Write a complete subject or complete predicate to complete each sentence.

Example: _____ *cut my hair.*
              My barber, Mr. Steve, cut my hair.

1. The next-door neighbor _____.

2. _____ bought a pair of hiking boots.

3. The dog and the cat _____.

4. Mr. Young's daughter _____.

5. _____ took their son to the park.

6. The usher at the movie theater _____.

7. _____ made a sculpture in art class.

8. _____ is my favorite TV show.

9. The yearbook committee _____.

10. _____ like jazz better than rock music.

Writing Application

Directions: Write five sentences below describing your family and what they do each day. Underline each complete subject once and each complete predicate twice.

_____

_____

_____

_____

_____

_____

_____

Name: _____   Date: _____

Unit 2: *Simple Subjects and Predicates*

In the **complete subject**, the **simple subject** is the main word telling whom or what the sentence is about.

The **simple subject** may be one word.

Example:

    <u>Bats</u> sleep during the day.

The **simple subject** may be several words that name a person or place.

Example:

    <u>George Washington</u> was the first President of the United States.

In the **complete predicate**, the **simple predicate** (or **verb**) is the main word that tells what the **subject** is or does.

Example:

    My dog <u>buried</u> his bone.

The simple predicate may be a main **verb** and a helping **verb**.

Example:

    Kayla <u>has sung</u> that song before.

Name: _____   Date: _____

Unit 2: *Identifying Simple Subjects and Predicates*

Practice

Directions: In each sentence, draw a slash between the complete subject and complete predicate. Then circle the simple subject and the simple predicate.

Example:

The ⟨man⟩ in the moon / ⟨is⟩ an imaginary character.

1. Another teacher is responsible for decorating the room.

2. Stewart and his mom visited me in the hospital.

3. Saul and Meghan have joined the science club.

4. Julia's flute was found in the hallway.

5. Everyone in my class knew the answer.

6. The three o'clock bell rang for dismissal.

7. Jerry and his dad drove to Mexico last summer.

8. Several team members were running extra laps.

9. Elvis Presley was known as the king of rock and roll.

10. Those two boys will help you carry that box.

11. My sister has the flu.

12. These trees have beautiful leaves in autumn.

Name: _____ Date: _____

Unit 2: *Simple Sentences*

Tip

A **simple sentence** is a sentence that contains one principal **independent clause** and no **subordinate clauses**. A **simple sentence** can be one word.

      Example: *Run! (subject is "you" understood)*

A **simple sentence** could also have a **compound subject**, **compound predicate**, an **appositive**, and **modifiers**.

      Example: *Daniel and Gail, our class representatives, are developing and organizing the teacher appreciation party after school.*

Practice

Directions: In each simple sentence below, underline the subject once and the verb or verb phrase twice.

      Example: *Allan and Jeffrey told me the answer.*

1. There are many days of school left.

2. George Mason, the new mailman, has a daughter.

3. My uncle got in his car, backed out, and left quickly.

4. Major Simon visited our classroom today.

5. Tracy Sterne, the school nurse, was absent.

6. I am buying my brother a book for Christmas.

7. We could see the forest fire down in the valley.

8. Cousin Albert is helping Dad in the bean field.

9. Chloe and Stacey are skating in New York.

10. Charles Lindbergh was the first pilot to fly alone and nonstop across the Atlantic.

Name: _____ Date: _____

Unit 2: *Compound Sentences*

Tip

If a **sentence** contains two or more main or **independent clauses**, it is a **compound sentence**.

    Example: *A severe storm is dangerous, but a tornado is dreadful.*

Main or **independent clauses** may be joined by using a **comma** and a **coordinating conjunction**.

    Example: *Do you plan to stay, or do you want to leave?*

Main or **independent clauses** may be joined by a **semicolon** if they are directly related.

    Example: *I could not see the play; people stood in front of me.*

Practice

Directions: Combine the sentence pairs using one of the methods above.

1. I did not see the television program. I did my homework.

    _____

    _____

2. Our coach was disappointed. The team felt bad.

    _____

    _____

3. Half the students in class were absent. Reports were given as usual.

    _____

    _____

4. You must practice your violin each day. You may have to sell it to someone.

    _____

    _____

Name: _____ Date: _____

Unit 2: *Creating Compound Sentences*

Practice

Directions: Change the following simple sentences into compound sentences.

1. His dream came true.

   _____

   _____

2. Andrea has a gift for helping others.

   _____

   _____

3. Connie is a science genius.

   _____

   _____

4. Our car stalled on Main Street.

   _____

   _____

5. Janet bought a new car.

   _____

   _____

6. Our house was dark and quiet.

   _____

   _____

7. Mom's soup was delicious.

   _____

   _____

8. The window on the van was broken.

   _____

   _____

Name: _____ Date: _____

Unit 2: *Clauses*

Tip

A **clause** is a group of words containing a **subject** and a **predicate**. It may contain an object, modifiers, and other words. It is also called an **independent clause**.

  Example: *My father was restless.*

A **dependent** or **subordinate clause** does not express a complete thought. It cannot stand alone. Look for **pronouns** like "who," "whom," "which," and "that." Also look for certain **conjunctions** that introduce **subordinate clauses** such as "after," "although," "because," "since," "unless," "when," and "where."

  Example: *when Andrew stepped off the plane*

Practice

Directions: Rewrite each sentence below, adding only punctuation and capitalization to independent clauses. For dependent clauses add an independent clause to make the thought complete. Also add capitalization and punctuation.

  Example: *when the sun shone brightly*
       The ice began to melt when the sun shone brightly.

1. from his vantage point

  _____

2. the man with the hat was smiling

  _____

3. within the pages of this book

  _____

4. the train arrived

  _____

5. although the bluebirds have returned

  _____

6. from Phoenix we returned to Flagstaff

  _____

Name: _____   Date: _____

Unit 2: *Finding Dependent Clauses*

Practice

Directions: Draw one line under any dependent clauses in the paragraph below. Not all sentences will have dependent clauses.

We had to leave after Sally finished her lunch. She was flying to her grandmother's house in Toledo. I helped her with her luggage when we arrived at the airport. Although Sally had never flown before, she acted like an old pro. She waited patiently for the time to board the plane. We toured the terminal as we waited for her flight to leave. She got something to eat, and I bought a magazine. While we waited, we read articles and worked puzzles. Sally finished one puzzle that she had started yesterday. We both got excited when we heard her flight number announced. Sally gathered her carry-on luggage and stepped in line. As she walked down the walkway to the plane, I waved frantically to her.

Writing Application

Directions: Write a paragraph on this topic: Describe your lunch break at school. What happens? Whom do you see? Use dependent clauses and underline them.

_____

_____

_____

_____

_____

_____

_____

_____

_____

Name: _____   Date: _____

Unit 2: *Using Dependent Clauses*

Tip

Dependent clauses can be **adjectives** or **adverbs** in their use.

Examples: *Did you write the story <u>that Anita read to the class</u>?*
                    modifies "story"

You may play chess <u>after you finish your chores</u>.
                    modifies "play"

Writing Application

Directions: Expand each simple sentence by adding the type of dependent clause indicated in parentheses.

1. (adverb) Ethan worked diligently. _____

    _____

2. (adjective) David began to describe the cave. _____

    _____

3. (adverb) We all laughed. _____

    _____

4. (adjective) Looking up at the ceiling, I spotted a hole. _____

    _____

5. (adverb) Rain began to pour. _____

    _____

6. (adjective) This is the exact spot. _____

    _____

7. (adverb) The game had already begun. _____

    _____

Name: _____ Date: _____

Unit 2: *Sentence Fragments*

Tip

A **sentence fragment** is an incomplete sentence, missing a **subject**, **predicate**, or both.

Incorrect:	*began to sound louder (needs a subject)*
	a passing car (needs a predicate)
	during the storm (needs both)
Correct:	*The horn began to sound louder.*
	A passing car sped right by us.
	My dog shook nervously during the storm.

Practice

Directions: Use the fragments below to create complete sentences of your own.

1. a great diplomat and statesman

   _____

   _____

2. without saying a word

   _____

   _____

3. two cases of oil and a filter

   _____

   _____

4. drove to town to see the doctor

   _____

   _____

5. convinced he was right

   _____

   _____

Name: _____   Date: _____

Unit 2: *Finding Fragments*

Practice

Directions: Read the article carefully. Underline only the sentence fragments you find. On the lines at the bottom, add the correct fragment from the selection to complete each thought.

In 1607 Virginia became the first southern colony. Known as the James River colony. The Indians in the neighborhood offered little trade. Soon the Indians. The English searched for gold mines and found none. Did not understand the soil of Virginia.

Though the owners of the Virginia colony in England were losing money. That the Pacific Ocean was only a few hundred miles away. John Smith was a sailor who may have been the only curious colonist. He stated later that his life was saved by the chief's daughter, Pocahontas. To keep peace with the Indians.

1. The colonists held together and formed a new charter _____

   _____

2. The few farmers _____

3. The colony's company thought _____

   _____

4. _____

   _____ Virginia started out successfully.

5. _____ became hostile.

6. Pocahontas was captured by the English _____

   _____

Name: _____   Date: _____

Unit 2: *Run-on Sentences*

Tip

      Correct **run-on sentences** by making two separate **sentences**, by using a **comma** and **conjunction**, by using a **coordinating conjunction**, or by using a **semicolon**.

Wrong: *Our PTO dinner will be Thursday the new members will be introduced.*

Right: *Our PTO dinner will be Thursday. The new members will be introduced. (two sentences)*

            Our PTO dinner will be Thursday; new members will be introduced. (semicolon)

            Our PTO dinner will be Thursday, and the new members will be introduced. (comma and conjunction)

Practice

Directions: Correct the run-on sentences below by using any of the four methods above. Do not use the same one each time. Try all four.

1. Military volunteers lacked experience so did most other soldiers.

   _____

   _____

2. The old man got nervous the phone rang again.

   _____

3. My dad had a flat he had four new tires.

   _____

4. Javier could not mow the yard the grass was too high.

   _____

5. The sun came out the road was still too muddy.

   _____

Name: _____ Date: _____

Unit 2: *Correcting Fragments and Run-on Sentences*

Practice

Directions: Read the sentences carefully. If you find no mistakes, write "correct" on the line. For fragments and run-on sentences, rewrite the sentence with proper corrections.

1. Brazil is full of natural wonders the Amazon River is just one.

   _____

   _____

2. The Amazon River runs through the world's largest rain forest.

   _____

   _____

3. Native Americans hunt and fish there their lives untouched by the modern world.

   _____

   _____

4. Brazil has fertile soil. That produces coffee, cocoa, and sugar cane.

   _____

   _____

5. The country has serious economic problems.

   _____

   _____

6. The Amazon rain forest is being destroyed. To make new farmland and grazing land.

   _____

   _____

Writing Application

Directions: Using your own paper, write on the following topic: What makes your best friend your best friend? Be specific and use complete sentences. Check for fragments and run-on sentences.

Name: _____ Date: _____

Unit 2: *Expanding Sentences*

Writing Application

Directions: Using exciting nouns and verbs, colorful adjectives and adverbs, and descriptive prepositional phrases and appositives, expand the following basic sentences.

Example: *I ran.*
              Afraid of the sound from the alley, I ran quickly to my neighbor's house.

1. We were walking.

    _____

    _____

2. Andrea turned.

    _____

    _____

3. The team watched.

    _____

    _____

4. Dion traced.

    _____

    _____

5. The lion stalked.

    _____

    _____

6. The wind blew.

    _____

    _____

7. Justin launched.

    _____

    _____

Name: _____   Date: _____

Unit 2: *Combining Sentences*

Tip

Avoid writing several short, choppy sentences. Vary your word order and join sentences to improve the rhythm and style of your writing.

Example:

Choppy: *Last Saturday Dad traded cars. He bought a blue SUV. He traded in our old one. It needed extensive repairs.*

Corrected: *Last Saturday Dad traded in our old car, which needed repairs, for a new, blue SUV.*

Practice

Directions: Rewrite the short sentences into more interesting, longer sentences.

1. Mother graduated from college. She attended Beloit College. She studied economics.

   _____

   _____

2. I will study after school. I will then watch television. I will watch college basketball.

   _____

   _____

3. I am reading a very good book. It is called Treasure Island. I got it from the library.

   _____

   _____

4. Jim worked hard last year. He taught his dog new tricks. He wanted to show the dog in competition.

   _____

   _____

   _____

Name: _____   Date: _____

Unit 2: *Misplaced and Dangling Modifiers*

Tip

Dangling modifiers are words or phrases that appear at the beginning of the sentence but fail to modify anything.

Example: *While being seated, the soup was served.*

You can change **dangling modifiers** in two ways. Change the subject of the sentence.

Example: *While being seated, <u>we</u> were served soup.*

Change the adjective phrase to an adverb clause.

Example: *While we were being seated, soup was served.*

Misplaced modifiers are adjectives or adverbs that, because of location, modify the wrong word.

Example: *Incorrect: Andrea was singing as she walked home at the top of her voice.*
Corrected: Andrea was singing at the top of her voice as she walked home.

Practice

Directions: Write the following sentences correctly by changing the dangling or misplaced modifiers.

1. Crying for attention, my aunt ignored the baby.

   _____

2. A table stood before the fireplace with carved legs.

   _____

3. Stepping inside the building, a jet was seen.

   _____

4. The teacher picked up the essay Kenny had written with a sigh.

   _____

   _____

Name: _____   Date: _____

Unit 2 Test 1: *Subjects and Predicates*

Directions: Darken the circle next to the words that correctly identify the underlined portion of each sentence.

Example: *Charlie is studying at the library.*

Ⓐ *simple subject*   Ⓑ *simple predicate*

Ⓒ *complete subject*   Ⓓ *complete predicate*

(B - "is studying" is the verb phrase)

1. Mother isn't here.
    Ⓐ simple subject   Ⓑ simple predicate
    Ⓒ complete subject   Ⓓ complete predicate

2. The little black kitten scratched the screen.
    Ⓐ simple subject   Ⓑ simple predicate
    Ⓒ complete subject   Ⓓ complete predicate

3. We divided the money between us.
    Ⓐ simple subject   Ⓑ simple predicate
    Ⓒ complete subject   Ⓓ complete predicate

4. I bought this bracelet for my aunt.
    Ⓐ simple subject   Ⓑ simple predicate
    Ⓒ complete subject   Ⓓ complete predicate

5. Dick and his dog ran down to the beach.
    Ⓐ simple subject   Ⓑ simple predicate
    Ⓒ complete subject   Ⓓ complete predicate

6. My sister Katie collects stamps.
    Ⓐ simple subject   Ⓑ simple predicate
    Ⓒ complete subject   Ⓓ complete predicate

7. Can you call me tomorrow?
    Ⓐ simple subject   Ⓑ simple predicate
    Ⓒ complete subject   Ⓓ complete predicate

8. Nitasha is swimming in the lake.
    Ⓐ simple subject   Ⓑ simple predicate
    Ⓒ complete subject   Ⓓ complete predicate

Name: _____ Date: _____

Unit 2 Test 2: *Fragments and Run-on Sentences*

Directions: Darken the circle next to the words that correctly label the word group as a fragment, a run-on, or a complete sentence.

Example: *Andrew, reaching across the table.*
Ⓐ *fragment*   Ⓑ *run-on*   Ⓒ *complete sentence*
(A - predicate is missing)

1.   The dog was trapped between fences.
Ⓐ fragment   Ⓑ run-on   Ⓒ complete sentence

2.   Andrew hit the ball it went over the wall.
Ⓐ fragment   Ⓑ run-on   Ⓒ complete sentence

3.   Stay here.
Ⓐ fragment   Ⓑ run-on   Ⓒ complete sentence

4.   Anchored in the harbor.
Ⓐ fragment   Ⓑ run-on   Ⓒ complete sentence

5.   Mr. Stone, the janitor of our building.
Ⓐ fragment   Ⓑ run-on   Ⓒ complete sentence

6.   May I sit here do you mind?
Ⓐ fragment   Ⓑ run-on   Ⓒ complete sentence

7.   Trent, living at home with his grandparents.
Ⓐ fragment   Ⓑ run-on   Ⓒ complete sentence

8.   Open the door for the teacher.
Ⓐ fragment   Ⓑ run-on   Ⓒ complete sentence

9.   Since I forgot my lunch.
Ⓐ fragment   Ⓑ run-on   Ⓒ complete sentence

10.   Leave!
Ⓐ fragment   Ⓑ run-on   Ⓒ complete sentence

Name: _____ Date: _____

Unit 2 Test 3: *Adjective and Adverb Clauses*

Directions: Darken the circle next to the words that correctly identify the underlined words as either an adjective clause or an adverb clause.

> **Example:**   *As he drove the car, he listened to the radio.*
>   Ⓐ *adjective clause*   🅑 *adverb clause*
>   *(B - describes when he listened)*

1. <u>Because the water was deep</u>, we were scared.
    Ⓐ adjective clause   Ⓑ adverb clause

2. <u>While the water was calm</u>, John rowed smoothly.
    Ⓐ adjective clause   Ⓑ adverb clause

3. It began to rain <u>while he was still speaking</u>.
    Ⓐ adjective clause   Ⓑ adverb clause

4. May I use the globe <u>that is on the table</u>?
    Ⓐ adjective clause   Ⓑ adverb clause

5. It was Jeanne <u>who phoned last night</u>.
    Ⓐ adjective clause   Ⓑ adverb clause

6. <u>As soon as the boat docked</u>, we headed for camp.
    Ⓐ adjective clause   Ⓑ adverb clause

7. <u>When Aunt Mary went shopping</u>, she lost her purse.
    Ⓐ adjective clause   Ⓑ adverb clause

8. Was that the story <u>that you told Mother</u>?
    Ⓐ adjective clause   Ⓑ adverb clause

9. This is the spot <u>where the pilgrims landed</u>.
    Ⓐ adjective clause   Ⓑ adverb clause

10. Marconi was the man <u>who invented the wireless telegraph</u>.
    Ⓐ adjective clause   Ⓑ adverb clause

Name: _____   Date: _____

Unit 3: "*About*," "*Off*," "*Of*," and "*Have*"

Tip

Don't use "at about" for "about."

> *Wrong:*   We begin practice <u>at about</u> four o'clock.
> *Right:*   We begin practice <u>about</u> four o'clock.

Don't use "off of" for "off."

> *Wrong:*   Mr. Jenkins' truck skidded <u>off of</u> the highway.
> *Right:*   Mr. Jenkins' truck skidded <u>off</u> the highway.

Don't use the preposition "of" in place of the helper "have."

> *Wrong:*   Heather should <u>of</u> known better.
> *Right:*   Heather should <u>have</u> known better.

Practice

Directions: Rewrite each incorrect sentence. If the sentence is correct, write a **C** on the line.

1. Take your books off of the piano.

   _____

2. Mr. Biloz's train arrives at about six o'clock.

   _____

3. Brittany should of finished her homework.

   _____

4. David fell off his bike.

   _____

5. We'll be there at about three o'clock.

   _____

6. Gabrielle must of decided not to go today.

   _____

7. A pencil rolled off of the desk.

   _____

Name: _____ Date: _____

Unit 3: *"Beside"* and *"Besides"*; *"Between"* and *"Among"*; and *"In"* and *"Into"*

Tip

"Beside" means "next to;" "besides" means "in addition to."

> *Tim is standing <u>beside</u> the pool.*
> *Who is leaving <u>besides</u> us?*

"Between" is used when its object refers to two things.
"Among" is used when its object refers to more than two.

> *The decision is <u>between</u> you and me.*
> *The decision is <u>among</u> all the class members.*

"In" means "within;" "into" means "from without to within."

> *What is <u>in</u> that box?*
> *Ciara dropped the worm <u>into</u> the box.*

Practice

Directions: Write the correct form of the word pair in parentheses in the sentence.

> **Example:** *Place your chair <u>beside</u> mine, Andrea. (beside, besides)*

1. We four people must keep the secret _____ ourselves. (between, among)

2. Put the burgers _____ the pan. (in, into)

3. What are we having for dinner _____ sweet corn? (beside, besides)

4. Craig, you need to sit _____ Cori and Brook. (between, among)

5. What do you have _____ that trunk? (in, into)

6. Leave the gift _____ the porch steps. (beside, besides)

7. Please pour the oil _____ a different container. (in, into)

8. You are _____ my best friends. (between, among)

Unit 3: *"Can" and "May"; "Good" and "Well"; and "It's" and "Its"*

Tip

"Can" means "to be able to."
"May" means "to have permission to."

> <u>Can</u> you find the right answer?
> You <u>may</u> watch television tonight.

"Good" is an **adjective** often used following a **linking verb** to modify the **subject**.
"Well" is an **adverb** telling "how." It can also be an **adjective** meaning "healthy."

> Mary's singing is <u>good</u>.
> Mary sings <u>well</u>.
> Mary feels <u>well</u>.

"It's" is the **contraction** for "it is."
"Its" is the **possessive pronoun**.

> <u>It's</u> time to go.
> The cat hurt <u>its</u> tail.

Practice

Directions: Insert into the sentence the correct form of the word pair.

1. How many sit-ups _____ you do? (can, may)

2. Geraldo skis _____. (good, well)

3. I think _____ your umbrella. (its, it's)

4. _____ we see the baby now? (Can, May)

5. This soup tastes _____. (good, well)

6. A bird takes _____ time bathing. (its, it's)

7. No one _____ leave before the bell rings. (can, may)

8. Bob writes _____ when he is interested. (good, well)

9. You know _____ not the truth. (its, it's)

10. Sarah said she did not feel _____. (good, well)

Name: _____ Date: _____

Unit 3: *"Sure" and "Surely"; "Nearly" and "Almost"*

Tip

The **adverb** "surely," not the **adjective** "sure," should be used to modify a verb, an adjective, or another adverb.

Wrong: Jim was <u>sure</u> glad to see his uncle.
Right: Jim was <u>surely</u> glad to see his uncle.

"Nearly" and "almost" are **adverbs**. "Near" and "most" should not be used in their place

Wrong: Ben <u>near</u> tripped on the rug.
Right: Ben <u>nearly</u> tripped on the rug.
Wrong: It is <u>most</u> time to go.
Right: It is <u>almost</u> time to go.

Practice

Directions: Circle the correct word for each sentence.

1. Jordan and Hailey were (almost, most) late for the bus.

2. Mr. Lewis (sure, surely) knows his hockey.

3. We were (near, nearly) hit by a car.

4. There are (most, almost) fifty bottles of soda left.

5. We (sure, surely) did a lot of work today.

6. I am (near, nearly) the end of the story.

7. You can be (sure, surely) that we will win the game.

8. This is the (most, almost) difficult test I've ever taken.

9. My brother is (near, nearly) fifty years old.

10. We were (sure, surely) happy to know that practice was canceled.

Name: _____ Date: _____

Unit 3: "*Than*" and "*As*"

Tip

You can use **subject** or **object pronouns** after "than" or "as" in **sentences** that compare one person to another. You can determine which **pronoun** case to use by expanding the **sentence** this way:

My dad is shorter than I.
My dad is shorter than I am.

Brock likes baseball more than me.
Brock likes baseball more than he likes me.
Brock likes baseball more than I.
Brock likes baseball more than I like baseball.

Practice

Directions: Circle the correct pronoun to complete each sentence. On the line below, expand the sentence to check your answer. If both pronouns are possible, expand both sentences.

1. Gary swims as well as (I, me)

_____

_____

2. Katie likes him better than (I, me).

_____

_____

3. Tiffany understands him better than (I, me).

_____

_____

4. Gage wrote a better letter than (she, her).

_____

_____

5. Sadie admires Mrs. Tavender more than (I, me).

_____

_____

Name: _____ Date: _____

Unit 3: *"Whose"* and *"Who's"*

Tip

"Whose" is a possessive **adjective**.
"Who's" is a **contraction** for "who is."

Example: *Whose idea was that?*
                 Who's the author of the book?

Practice

Directions: On the line in each sentence, write either "whose" or "who's."

1. _____ CD did you borrow?

2. _____ the captain of your team?

3. I know _____ birthday is today.

4. _____ turn is it to collect the equipment?

5. _____ car is parked outside?

6. _____ the best artist in class?

7. _____ horse is running loose?

8. That is the policeman _____ wife teaches.

9. _____ cleaning the upstairs?

10. The player _____ glove is on the ground has been taken from the field.

11. _____ coming for supper?

12. _____ going to the game tonight?

13. I don't know _____ qualified for the job.

14. _____ responsible for this situation?

15. _____ phone number is on this pager?

Name: _____ Date: _____

Unit 3: *"They're," "There," and "Their"*

Tip

"They're" is a **contraction** for "they are."
I know they're always at home at this time.

"There" is an **adverb** meaning "at that point."
Place the sofa over there.

"Their" is the **possessive** form of "they."
I knew their house was for sale.

Practice

Directions: Write either "they're," "their," or "there" in the spaces below.

1. _____ has to be a better way.

2. You can't really believe _____ story.

3. I believe _____ my best friends.

4. I never go _____ for breakfast.

5. _____ in trouble with the principal.

6. It is not _____ address that I need.

7. We must give them a ride to _____ farm.

8. I heard _____ related to you.

Writing Application

Directions: Write original sentences using the words in parentheses.

1. (their) _____

2. (there) _____

3. (they're) _____

Name: _____   Date: _____

Unit 3: *"Then" and "Than"*

Tip

"Than" is a **conjunction**.
"Then" is an **adverb**.

Example: *She feels better this week than last week.*
                Then she raised her hand and gave the answer.

Practice

Directions: Use "than" or "then" to correctly complete each sentence.

1. I understand it better today _____ yesterday.

2. It must be my turn _____.

3. Finish the test, _____ go out to recess.

4. It seems much darker _____ I thought.

5. They knew it _____; they know it now.

6. Helium is lighter _____ air.

7. A killer whale is larger _____ a dolphin.

8. That was _____; this is now.

9. I knew better _____ to ask her a question.

10. My job is easier _____ my brother's job.

Writing Application

Directions: Write original sentences using the words in parentheses.

1. (than) _____

2. (then) _____

Name: _____   Date: _____

Unit 3: *"Your"* and *"You're"*

Tip

"You're" is a **contraction** of "you are."
"Your" is a possessive **pronoun**.

Example: *You're* the best grandfather ever.
We know *your* phone number.

Practice

Directions: Use either "your" or "you're" to complete the sentences.

1. I can tell _____ scared.

2. _____ not to check out a book.

3. I heard _____ project was a winner.

4. If _____ sure you can, let me know.

5. This may be _____ last chance to go.

6. _____ wanted in the main office.

7. _____ trumpet is in the hall.

8. You know _____ always welcome here.

9. _____ not the only athlete on the honor roll.

10. You must not lose _____ temper during the game.

Writing Application

Directions: Write original sentences using the words in parentheses.

1. (you're) _____

2. (your) _____

Name: _____ Date: _____

Unit 3 Test: *Usage*

Directions: Darken the circle next to the line that has an error in usage. Darken "D" if no correction is needed.

Example:
    Ⓐ *Please put your*
    ⬤ *box of paints besides*
    Ⓒ *the good table.*
    Ⓓ *no error*
    (B - should be "beside")

1. Ⓐ My brother then
    Ⓑ fell into the pond
    Ⓒ among the two trees.
    Ⓓ no error

2. Ⓐ You surely know
    Ⓑ how to sing better
    Ⓒ than my sister.
    Ⓓ no error

3. Ⓐ It took near
    Ⓑ two weeks for the
    Ⓒ dog to shed its hair.
    Ⓓ no error

4. Ⓐ Can you tell me
    Ⓑ how good your
    Ⓒ television gets channel ten?
    Ⓓ no error

5. Ⓐ It's the best
    Ⓑ restaurant among
    Ⓒ all in our city.
    Ⓓ no error

6. Ⓐ May Steve please
    Ⓑ call your office
    Ⓒ at about two o'clock?
    Ⓓ no error

7. Ⓐ Tell me whose
    Ⓑ team nearly made
    Ⓒ you're top ten.
    Ⓓ no error

8. Ⓐ May I clean
    Ⓑ the tape off of
    Ⓒ the chalkboard?
    Ⓓ no error

9. Ⓐ They're better
    Ⓑ trombone players then
    Ⓒ their conference rivals.
    Ⓓ no error

10. Ⓐ Who's the best
    Ⓑ artist between the
    Ⓒ three of you?
    Ⓓ no error

Name: _____   Date: _____

Unit 3 Test: *Usage (Continued)*

11. Ⓐ You can enter
    Ⓑ the poster contest
    Ⓒ if you're ready.
    Ⓓ no error

12. Ⓐ I know well
    Ⓑ that there the
    Ⓒ students to blame.
    Ⓓ no error

13. Ⓐ Only one person
    Ⓑ besides me was
    Ⓒ invited into the Honors Club.
    Ⓓ no error

14. Ⓐ Beside Sheila,
    Ⓑ there were two other
    Ⓒ girls in the play.
    Ⓓ no error

15. Ⓐ She should of
    Ⓑ gone home
    Ⓒ right after school.
    Ⓓ no error

16. Ⓐ I am sure that
    Ⓑ your bread tastes
    Ⓒ better than mine.
    Ⓓ no error

17. Ⓐ Jason near walked
    Ⓑ into the tree
    Ⓒ before he stopped.
    Ⓓ no error

18. Ⓐ Is Kyra as
    Ⓑ short as
    Ⓒ me?
    Ⓓ no error

19. Ⓐ Jamal can run
    Ⓑ faster than
    Ⓒ I.
    Ⓓ no error

20. Ⓐ He is coming
    Ⓑ to dinner
    Ⓒ at about six o'clock.
    Ⓓ no error

Name: _____ Date: _____

Unit 4: *Prefixes*

Tip

A **prefix** is placed at the beginning of a word to change the meaning. Some common **prefixes** are:

ad - to	**de** - down	**post** - after
pre - before	**sub** - under	**trans** - across
anti - against	**ex** - out	**in** - not
mis - wrong	**non** - not	**super** - above

Writing Application

Directions: Add one of the prefixes above to each word in parentheses. Then write an original sentence using the word correctly.

Example: *(spell)* <u>misspell</u>   *Don't misspell another word.*

1. (sonic)   _____

   _____

2. (conscious)   _____

   _____

3. (mature)   _____

   _____

4. (continental) _____

   _____

5. (violent)   _____

   _____

6. (visible)   _____

   _____

7. (absorbent)   _____

   _____

Name: _____ Date: _____

Unit 4: *Suffixes*

Tip

A **suffix** is placed at the end of a word. Some common suffixes are:

able - can be	**less** - without	**er** - one who does
ness - quality of	**ish** - like, somewhat	**ful** - full of

Writing Application

Directions: Add one of the suffixes above to each word in parentheses. Then write an original sentence using the word correctly.

Example: *(like)* <u>likable</u>   *She is a likable young lady.*

1. (help)   _____

   _____

2. (child)   _____

   _____

3. (gentle)   _____

   _____

4. (read)   _____

   _____

5. (hope)   _____

   _____

6. (play)   _____

   _____

7. (green)   _____

   _____

8. (color)   _____

   _____

9. (fool)   _____

   _____

10. (kind)   _____

   _____

Name: _____ Date: _____

Unit 4: *Using Suffixes and Prefixes*

Writing Application

Directions: Using your own paper, write a paragraph using each prompt below. Make sure you use at least one word containing a prefix and one word containing a suffix. Underline the words.

Prompt 1:

Explain how you could entertain your whole family without spending any money.

Prompt 2:

What three words would describe you? Explain each one carefully and support each with facts.

Prompt 3:

Describe a time when someone really scared you. What happened? How did you feel?

Prompt 4:

What country other than America would you most want to visit? Why?

Prompt 5:

If your pet (or someone else's pet) could talk, what do you think it would tell you? Be specific in your explanation.

Name: _____ Date: _____

Unit 4: *Metaphors*

Tip

A **metaphor** compares two different things without using the words "like" or "as."

Example: *The linebacker was a bull on the football field.*
(The linebacker and a bull are being compared in strength.)

Practice

Directions: In the metaphors below, underline the two very different things being compared. Then on the line explain how they are being compared.

Example: *The sun was a diamond in the sky.*
The sun was as bright as a diamond.

1. Adrian proved to be the bad apple of the group.

   _____

2. I wanted to be the big wheel in the club.

   _____

3. My mother was a busy bee yesterday.

   _____

4. The rock singer's fans were sharks in the ocean after the concert.

   _____

5. The highway was a silver ribbon in the moonlight.

   _____

6. My brother is the king of clichés.

   _____

7. My uncle's new car is a real lemon.

   _____

8. As soon as swimming lessons started, she became a little fish.

   _____

Name: _____   Date: _____

Unit 4: *Similes*

Tip

A **simile** compares two very different things using the words "like" or "as."

Example: *The volunteer worker was like an angel to us.*
(both are surprising helpers)

Practice

Directions: Underline the objects being compared in each sentence and circle the "like" or "as." On the line explain how the objects are being compared.

1. The wet carpet was as soft as a sponge.

   _____

2. Dee was so embarrassed, she looked like a beet.

   _____

3. Bob was very scared; his legs were like gelatin.

   _____

4. From the air, the houses looked like shoe boxes fitted together.

   _____

5. The sprinter was like the wind.

   _____

6. My anger was as explosive as a grenade.

   _____

7. Mrs. Charlson's voice was like a foghorn.

   _____

Name: _____ Date: _____

Unit 4: *Writing Similes and Metaphors*

Writing Application

Directions: Finish the sentences below by completing the simile or metaphor in each.

1. Although he was little, his heart was like _____

   _____

2. The final days of Christmas vacation vanished like _____

   _____

3. Tonya's sadness was like _____

   _____

4. Michelle's smile radiates like _____

   _____

5. I thought that novel was about as interesting as _____

   _____

6. The traffic in town was as slow as _____

   _____

7. The tall grass in our yard was _____

   _____

8. That road through the mountains is as dangerous as _____

   _____

9. My cousin's old truck was like _____

   _____

10. The rolls at the restaurant were _____

    _____

_____   _____

Name: _____ Date: _____

Unit 4: *Double Negatives*

Tip

Do not use more than one **negative** word in the same sentence. Do not use a **negative** in a sentence with "hardly," "barely," or "scarcely." Also, the words "no," "none," "never," "nobody," "nowhere," and "nothing" are negative along with the word "not."

Wrong: I don't have <u>no</u> money.
Right: I don't have any money.
Right: I do have <u>no</u> money.

Practice

Directions: Rewrite the sentences correcting the double negatives in each.

1. Stacey hasn't no interest in that topic.

    _____

2. I can't hardly wait until the bell rings.

    _____

3. The counselors can't do nothing about the schedule.

    _____

4. There wasn't no light in the room.

    _____

5. Haven't you never seen this film before?

    _____

6. There hasn't been nothing sent to our pen pals.

    _____

7. Debbie barely had no time to get to school.

    _____

8. I couldn't hear nothing in that basement.

    _____

9. Won't nobody help me with this box?

    _____

10. Sheila won't tell nobody the reason.

    _____

11. They simply don't know no better.

    _____

Name: _____ Date: _____

Unit 4: *Avoiding Double Negatives*

Writing Application

Directions: Convert the following sentences to negative statements. Remember to avoid double negatives. Include the word in parentheses.

> **Example:** *Brittany has a pen today.*
> *Brittany has no pen today. (no)*
> *Brittany hasn't a pen today. (not)*

1. I have relatives in town. (no)

   _____

2. You can tell the difference in his appearance. (scarcely)

   _____

3. Our minister found us at home last night. (not)

   _____

4. You can see the tower from here. (hardly)

   _____

5. I did something to help that family. (nothing)

   _____

6. I know him very well. (scarcely)

   _____

7. I did something. (nothing)

   _____

8. They could see through the thick fog. (hardly)

   _____

9. I do have questions about the story. (not)

   _____

10. Does anybody know the combination to this lock? (nobody)

    _____

Name: _____   Date: _____

Unit 4 Test 1: *Prefixes and Suffixes*

Directions: Darken the circle for the word that has either a suffix or a prefix. Darken "D" if the answer is not given.

Example: *Which word has a prefix?*
Ⓐ *unanswered* Ⓑ *lifetime* Ⓒ *owner's* Ⓓ *none*
(A - unanswered means "not answered")

1. *Which word has a suffix?*
   Ⓐ fright   Ⓑ take   Ⓒ return   Ⓓ none

2. *Which word has a prefix?*
   Ⓐ collection   Ⓑ misleading   Ⓒ value   Ⓓ none

3. *Which word has a suffix?*
   A renew   Ⓑ stem   Ⓒ entertainment   Ⓓ none

4. *Which word has a prefix?*
   Ⓐ cheese   Ⓑ antivirus   Ⓒ statement   Ⓓ none

5. *Which word has a suffix?*
   Ⓐ friendship   Ⓑ prerecord   Ⓒ game   Ⓓ none

6. *Which word has a prefix?*
   Ⓐ collect   Ⓑ imperfect   Ⓒ stairs   Ⓓ none

7. *Which word has a suffix?*
   Ⓐ hotel   Ⓑ unconscious   Ⓒ notable   Ⓓ none

8. *Which word has a prefix?*
   Ⓐ detour   Ⓑ rack   Ⓒ leading   Ⓓ none

9. *Which word has a suffix?*
   Ⓐ untidy   Ⓑ generally   Ⓒ book   Ⓓ none

10. *Which word has a prefix?*
    Ⓐ calendar   Ⓑ nonstop   Ⓒ lovable   Ⓓ none

Name: _____   Date: _____

Unit 4 Test 2: *Similes and Metaphors*

Directions: Darken the circle next to the word that identifies the sentence as either a metaphor or a simile. Darken "C" if the answer is not given.

Example: *The defensive end stood tall, an oak tree among men.*
   Ⓐ *simile*   Ⓑ *metaphor*   Ⓒ *none*

1. That strip of bacon was as hot as a coal.
   Ⓐ simile   Ⓑ metaphor   Ⓒ none

2. The moon was a silver dollar in the sky.
   Ⓐ simile   Ⓑ metaphor   Ⓒ none

3. My uncle was stunned, a statue standing alone.
   Ⓐ simile   Ⓑ metaphor   Ⓒ none

4. Trish owns three beautiful kittens.
   Ⓐ simile   Ⓑ metaphor   Ⓒ none

5. My sister's mouth was like the Colorado River.
   Ⓐ simile   Ⓑ metaphor   Ⓒ none

6. The flashlight glowed like a beacon in the night.
   Ⓐ simile   Ⓑ metaphor   Ⓒ none

7. The people on the bus were dummies wearing a variety of masks.
   Ⓐ simile   Ⓑ metaphor   Ⓒ none

8. Carl played a wonderful game at goalie.
   Ⓐ simile   Ⓑ metaphor   Ⓒ none

9. Police cars moved quietly like ants around their hill.
   Ⓐ simile   Ⓑ metaphor   Ⓒ none

10. My granddaughter was an angel all night long.
    Ⓐ simile   Ⓑ metaphor   Ⓒ none

Name: _____   Date: _____

Unit 4 Test 3: *Double Negatives*

Directions: Darken the circle next to the sentence that demonstrates the use of a double negative.

Example: Ⓐ *I couldn't hardly wait.*
Ⓑ *I could hardly wait.*
Ⓒ *I couldn't wait.*
(A - "not" and "hardly")

1. Ⓐ Nancy doesn't have time.
Ⓑ Nancy does have no time.
Ⓒ Nancy doesn't have no time.

2. Ⓐ Millie has no homework.
Ⓑ Millie hasn't no homework.
Ⓒ Millie hasn't any homework.

3. Ⓐ Mother hasn't bought nothing.
Ⓑ Mother has bought nothing.
Ⓒ Mother hasn't bought anything.

4. Ⓐ Isn't anybody watching the game?
Ⓑ Is anybody watching the game?
Ⓒ Isn't nobody watching the game?

5. Ⓐ Didn't none of them have tickets for the circus?
Ⓑ Did none of them have tickets for the circus?
Ⓒ Didn't any of them have tickets for the circus?

6. Ⓐ There aren't any children in the neighborhood.
Ⓑ There are no children in the neighborhood.
Ⓒ There aren't no children in the neighborhood.

7. Ⓐ Ted hasn't had any luck.
Ⓑ Ted hasn't had no luck.
Ⓒ Ted has had no luck.

Name: _____ Date: _____

Unit 5: *Capitalization*

Tip

1. **Capitalize** geographic names: cities, states, countries, rivers, bodies of water, mountains, islands, and so on.

    Examples: *Milwaukee, Wisconsin*   *Lake Erie*

2. **Capitalize** the names of churches, schools, monuments, public buildings, parks, and streets.

    Examples: *Empire State Building*   *Forty-second Street*

3. **Capitalize** the names of organizations, government agencies, and business firms.

    Examples: *the American Red Cross*   *the Boy Scouts of America*

4. **Capitalize** the names of holidays, historical events, and historical documents.

    Examples: *Fourth of July*   *the Magna Carta*

5. **Capitalize** the first word, the last word, and each important word in a title of a book, magazine, poem, story, newspaper, movie, play, or television program. Underline the titles of longer works such as books, plays, magazines, movies, and newspapers. Put quotation marks around smaller works such as articles, poems, songs, and television shows.

    Examples: *A Tale of Two Cities* (book)
    "The Cosby Show" (television show)
    Hamlet (play)
    "Stopping by Woods on a Snowy Evening" (poem)

6. **Capitalize** the names of races, religions, and nationalities, whether used as adjectives or nouns.

    Examples: *England*   *English*
    Indiana   *Lutheran*

7. **Capitalize** all abbreviations of words that would be capitalized if spelled out.

    Examples: *Mr. Anderson*   *Dr. Drake*
    Chicago, IL   *Nov. 8*

Name: _____   Date: _____

Unit 5: *Capitalization Practice*

Practice

Directions: Rewrite each sentence, making corrections in capitalization.

1. I am collecting for easter seals this year.

   _____

2. We camped at duncan park in indiana.

   _____

3. Steve borrowed the adventures of tom sawyer from the library.

   _____

   _____

4. The ohio river empties into the mississippi river.

   _____

5. The constitution replaced the articles of confederation.

   _____

6. We saw mount rainier in washington.

   _____

7. I attended douglas high school on fulton avenue.

   _____

8. We have no school on columbus day and veterans' day.

   _____

   _____

9. They saw the statue of liberty on liberty island in new york.

   _____

   _____

10. I had to read call of the wild for a report.

    _____

Name: _____ Date: _____

Unit 5: *More Capitalization Practice*

Practice

Directions: If the sentence has no errors in capitalization, write "C" on the line. If an uppercase letter should be lowercase, or a lowercase letter should be uppercase, write an "I" on the line and make the correction in the sentence.

                                            D

Example: *I*   Tom delivers the ⓓaily Globe each day.

1. _____ My parents were married on Memorial day.

2. _____ Are the Philippine islands in the Pacific Ocean or Indian Ocean?

3. _____ Several people have swum the English Channel.

4. _____ I have a pen pal in Paris, France.

5. _____ My uncle works for the Department Of The Interior.

6. _____ I would like to attend Southwest Missouri State university.

7. _____ My birthday is in August.

8. _____ I have Canadian friends, but they don't speak french.

9. _____ The Declaration Of Independence is in Washington, D.C.

10. _____ Mr. Douglas works for Atkins, Inc.

11. _____ We will vacation near the Gulf Of Mexico.

12. _____ My parents watched "the brady bunch."

13. _____ I believe Mark Twain wrote the novel Life On The Mississippi.

Name: _____ Date: _____

Unit 5: *Capitalization Crossword*

Directions: Read each sentence carefully. Find the word that represents an error in capitalization. Write that word in the corresponding puzzle box.

ACROSS

2. Toronto is a City in Canada.
4. I enjoy french art and Italian cars.
5. My aunt lives in Puerto rico.
7. Many Americans listen to spanish music.
9. Have you caught a bass out of apple Creek?

DOWN

1. Is the Doctor at Williams Hospital?
3. Hawaii has several Islands.
4. My uncle was born on the fourth of July.
6. Jefferson High School starts in the Fall.
8. Harrisburg is the Capital of Pennsylvania.

Name: _____   Date: _____

Unit 5: *End Punctuation*

Tip

A **period** ends a **declarative sentence**.
> **Example:** *Our paper boy was late again.*

A **period** also ends an **imperative sentence**.
> **Example:** *Enter the room, please.*

A **question mark** ends an **interrogative sentence**.
> **Example:** *What is going on?*

An **exclamation point** ends an **exclamatory sentence**.
> **Example:** *What a great game!*

Practice

Directions: Place the proper punctuation mark at the end of each sentence.

1. Please close the door

2. How devastating that storm was

3. What does the doll cost, Allie

4. Were you looking for these papers

5. Look out

6. Eat your dinner

7. What a beautiful day

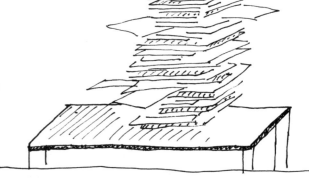

Directions: Complete the list of "favorites" below. Be sure to capitalize correctly.
Write the name of your favorite:

1. TV show _____

2. holiday _____

3. month _____

4. city _____

5. song _____

6. book _____

Name: _____   Date: _____

Unit 5: *Commas*

Tip

1. Use a **comma** to set off "yes," "no," "oh," and "well" at the beginning of a sentence.

    Example: *No, James was not home.*

2. Use a **comma** (or **commas**) to set off a word in direct address.

    Example: *Do you know, Tiffany, where the atlas is?*

3. Use a **comma** (or **commas**) to set off an **appositive** or appositive phrase, unless the appositive is so closely connected with the word it follows that it restricts its meaning.

    Examples: *Mr. Brinkman, our custodian, is leaving.*
    I read the novel <u>Huckleberry Finn</u>.

4. Use a **comma** (or **commas**) to set off parenthetical words and expressions—words that interrupt the main thought of the sentence.

    Example: *This story, in my opinion, is the author's best.*

5. Use **commas** to separate words or groups of words in a series.

    Example: *Allen, Brett, and Leah brought candy, cupcakes, and chips.*

6. Use **commas** to separate the items in a date or an address.

    Example: *She was born Saturday, June 3, 1989, in Memphis, Tennessee.*

7. In a compound sentence, separate the main independent clauses by placing a **comma** before the coordinating conjunctions.

    Example: *The sky was clear and bright, but a gloom hung over the stadium.*

8. Use a **comma** to separate two or more descriptive adjectives preceding a noun if "and" could have been used to join them. Use **commas** also to set off adjectives that follow a noun they modify.

    Examples: *The wild, hungry tiger paced through the grass.*
    The tiger, wild and hungry, paced through the grass.

Name: _____ Date: _____

Unit 5: *Comma Practice*

Practice

Directions: Insert commas where they are needed in these sentences.

1. May we go to the movie Mother?

2. Yes if your brother goes with you.

3. Just in case Ramon asked him first.

4. We are reading April Morning a novel by Howard Fast.

5. Our school as you know has a new computer lab.

6. For example each math problem must be written out.

7. Mr. Royster the new history teacher has two children.

8. I passed English geography math and science.

9. Her address is 910 Hall Drive Rockford Illinois.

10. Ashley cooked the steak and Jared poured the soda.

11. When the bell finally rings get in line quietly.

12. That quiet restored engine runs great.

13. Staring at the road the policeman began to write the ticket.

14. My brother was born on October 1 1981.

15. The boys tired and hungry staggered into the house.

16. Monica where is Danielle's coat?

17. Although the sun was shining the air was cool.

18. Most of the players however were on the bus.

19. Andrew Jackson in my opinion was a good President.

20. On May 18 1992 the store opened its doors for the first time.

Name: _____ Date: _____

Unit 5: *Using Commas*

Writing Application

Directions: Write original sentences using commas as directed by the words in parentheses.

Example: *(items in a series)* <u>We left without coats, hats, and gloves.</u>

1. (introductory "Oh") _____

    _____

2. (noun of direct address) _____

    _____

3. (an appositive) _____

    _____

4. (interrupting words) _____

    _____

5. (items in a series) _____

    _____

6. (items in a date) _____

    _____

7. (items in an address) _____

    _____

8. (compound sentence with conjunction) _____

    _____

9. (complex sentence with introductory adverb clause) _____

    _____

Name: _____ Date: _____

Unit 5: *Semicolons and Colons*

Tip

Semicolons and **colons**, like commas, must be used carefully.

A **semicolon** separates the clauses of a **compound sentence** when they are not joined by a coordinating conjunction.

Example: *Our band was ecstatic; they won a first place at contest.*

A **colon** separates the minutes from the hour when time is expressed in numbers.

Example: *Meet me tomorrow morning at 7:45.*

A **colon** is also used to precede a list of items that rename a word before the **colon**.

Example: *The following awards will be presented: attendance, spelling, PE, and history.*

Practice

Directions: Add a colon or semicolon to the sentences below.

1. My bus arrives at 7 30 each morning.

2. It has been dry for weeks farmers are hauling water.

3. These are my favorite teams the Jets, the Dodgers, the Flyers, and the Celtics.

4. David had better hurry he will be late if he's not careful.

5. The following people should report to the office Dante, Greg, and Felipe.

6. Suddenly Steve noticed the rattlesnake he couldn't move a muscle.

7. Fly-fishing has great appeal however, I like to use lures.

8. Only one other possibility remains travel by bus.

Name: _____   Date: _____

Unit 5: *Quotation Marks*

Tip

When you write what a person said but do not use the exact words, you are using an **indirect quotation**. An **indirect quotation** requires no special punctuation.

       Example: *Carly said that she has choir practice.*

A **direct quotation** is the exact words of a speaker and requires **quotation marks**.

       Example: *Carly said, "I have choir practice."*

Notice the use of periods and commas with the following examples of **direct quotations.**

       Examples: *"I have choir practice," Carly said.*
                       "I have," Carly said, "choir practice tonight."
                       "I have choir practice," Carly said. "Meet me there."

Practice

Directions: Punctuate these sentences, inserting quotation marks, commas, periods, question marks, and capital letters where needed.

1. That was a great catch Steven said the coach

2. Devinn asked has anyone seen my books

3. Scram shouted the store owner

4. If you go with me Sandy said I will buy your lunch

5. Open the window requested Mrs. Phillips

6. My grandfather said Gloria lives in Utah

7. The umpire shouted safe

8. My report is ready said Lee it is about rocks

Name: _____   Date: _____

Unit 5: *Writing With Quotation Marks*

Tip

Quotation marks enclose **direct quotations**. Some things to remember about using **quotation marks:**
1. Periods and commas go inside quotation marks.
2. Colons and semicolons go outside quotation marks.
3. Exclamation points and question marks usually go inside quotation marks.
4. A new paragraph begins with every change of speaker.

Writing Application

Directions: Read the conversation below. Carefully study the quotation marks and other punctuation. Also notice the paragraphing. Next, complete the conversation with your own original material.

"Can you tell me," said Nicci, "which of these two doors goes to the basement?"

"I don't know," replied Tiffany. "I think it's the door on the north."

"What's down there?" asked Nicci.

"I don't have a clue," answered Tiffany. "I thought I heard sounds from there, though."

"I think I'll go down there myself," boasted Nicci.

"I don't think you should. Wait, Nicci! Don't go," exclaimed Tiffany. "What? What did you say?"

_____

_____

_____

_____

_____

_____

_____

_____

_____

_____

Name: _____   Date: _____

Unit 5: *Titles*

Tip

Use **quotation marks** around titles of poems, short stories, articles, and songs.

      Example: *Poem: "Concord Bridge"*

Underline the titles of longer works such as books, magazines, plays, motion pictures, and newspapers.

      Example: *Movie: Top Gun*

Practice

Directions: Punctuate the following titles correctly.

1. Victory (book) _____

2. The Raven (poem) _____

3. The Open Boat (short story) _____

4. The Adventures of Tom Sawyer (book) _____

5. Time (magazine) _____

6. Across Five Aprils (book) _____

7. The Riddle (play) _____

8. The Necklace (short story) _____

9. Daily Globe (newspaper) _____

10. Surfing (magazine article) _____

11. Shipwrecked (movie) _____

12. Atlanta Constitution (newspaper) _____

Name: _____ Date: _____

Unit 5: *Writing Titles*

Writing Application

Directions: Write a title for each of the following. Remember to punctuate and capitalize correctly.

1. a book _____

2. a short poem _____

3. a magazine _____

4. a play _____

5. a short story _____

6. a song _____

7. a newspaper _____

8. a magazine _____

Directions: Rewrite the sentences below using correct punctuation.

1. Have you ever read the book A Bell for Adano?

   _____

2. I took my cousin to rent the movie Titanic.

   _____

3. I enjoy singing Happy Birthday.

   _____

4. My uncle subscribes to the magazine The Sign.

   _____

5. Who wrote the story The Great Stone Face?

   _____

Name: _____ Date: _____

Unit 5: *Apostrophes*

Tip

Use **apostrophes** to show possessive nouns.

> **Example:** *What is Tara's address?*

Use apostrophes in **contractions** to show that one or more letters has been omitted.

> **Example:** *That's the song I heard last night.*

Use **apostrophes** with an "s" to form the plural of a letter, a number, or a symbol.

> **Examples:** *three t's   four 3's   two +'s*

Practice

Directions: On the lines below, rewrite any sentence with at least one apostrophe error in it. Make the correction. If a sentence has no error, write "C" for correct.

1. I found three b's written on Williams paper.

   _____

2. Is this you're jacket, Sidney?

   _____

3. I don't know where Nick's books are.

   _____

4. Isn't this your brothers car?

   _____

5. We werent able to wash Mr. Johnsons truck.

   _____

6. Don't make your o's look like a's.

   _____

7. Its in the hall closet.

   _____

8. Who's bicycle was Steve riding?

   _____

Name: _____   Date: _____

Unit 5: *Using Apostrophes*

Writing Application

Directions: Write your own original sentences using correctly the word or words in parentheses.

Example: *(+'s) You left out the +'s in your math problems.*

1. (it's) _____

2. (you're) _____

3. (who's) _____

4. (your) _____

5. (doesn't) _____

6. (its) _____

7. (whose) _____

8. (they're) _____

9. (boy's) _____

10. (boys') _____

Writing Application

Directions: Write a paragraph on your own paper describing a place you have visited that you would love to revisit very soon. Explain why you would like to return. Use correctly examples of at least two of the three apostrophe rules.

Name: _____   Date: _____

Unit 5: *Capitalization and Punctuation Review*

Practice

Directions: Rewrite the following sentences using correct punctuation and capitalization.

> **Example:** *color photography was developed by auguste and louis lumiere on january 3 1907.*
>
> *Color photography was developed by Auguste and Louis Lumiere on January 3, 1907.*

1. in february of 1916 americans were first introduced to windshield wipers.

   _____

   _____

2. charles lindbergh on march 14 1927 made his great nonstop solo flight across the atlantic ocean.

   _____

   _____

3. on april 24 1939 german and soviet forces occupied poland, starting ww II.

   _____

   _____

4. the great jackie robinson broke the race barrier in major league baseball on may 8 1947.

   _____

   _____

5. the first artificial satellite sputnik I was launched by the soviets on october 4 1957.

   _____

   _____

6. in august of 1968 rev dr martin luther king jr. was assassinated in memphis tennessee.

   _____

   _____

Name: _____   Date: _____

Unit 5: *Comma Review*

Writing Application

Directions: Write an original sentence using the comma rule in parentheses.

      Example: *(a mild, introductory interjection)*   <u>*Well, no one told me to leave early.*</u>

1. (back-to-back introductory prepositional phrases) _____

     _____

2. (four direct objects in a series) _____

     _____

3. (separate two sentences with a conjunction) _____

     _____

4. (three subjects in a series) _____

     _____

5. (introductory adverb clause) _____

     _____

6. (an appositive) _____

     _____

7. (day and date, month, and year in the middle of the sentence) _____

     _____

8. (direct quotation) _____

     _____

9. (city and state in the middle of a sentence) _____

     _____

10. (three verbs in a series) _____

     _____

Name: _____ Date: _____

Unit 5 Test 1: *Capitalization*

Directions: Darken the circle next to the line containing an error in capitalization. Darken "D" if no error exists.

Example: Ⓐ *Has Kelly been to*
⬤Ⓑ *the Jones library to*
Ⓒ *get* Call of the Wild*?*
Ⓓ *none*

(B - Jones Library - the name of the library)

1. Ⓐ I read The Virginian,
   Ⓑ a novel by Owen Wister,
   Ⓒ for History class.
   Ⓓ none

2. Ⓐ I believe Mother
   Ⓑ will ask your mother
   Ⓒ to visit David Art gallery.
   Ⓓ none

3. Ⓐ The house on East
   Ⓑ Street belongs to
   Ⓒ Dr. Evans and his family.
   Ⓓ none

4. Ⓐ Paul Revere rode through
   Ⓑ Boston informing the people
   Ⓒ that the british were coming.
   Ⓓ none

5. Ⓐ My Uncle Dennis was
   Ⓑ born on the West Coast, but
   Ⓒ my Aunt was born in the Bahamas.
   Ⓓ none

6. Ⓐ Mr. Duffy lives at
   Ⓑ 222 East Bridgeport
   Ⓒ in Toledo, ohio.
   Ⓓ none

Name: _____   Date: _____

Unit 5 Test 1: *Capitalization (Continued)*

7. Ⓐ Next Thursday is
   Ⓑ Veterans' day, a holiday
   Ⓒ to honor great Americans.
   Ⓓ none

8. Ⓐ After President Warren
   Ⓑ Harding died, Calvin Coolidge
   Ⓒ became the thirtieth president.
   Ⓓ none

9. Ⓐ On July 15, John and
   Ⓑ Walter camped at Mount
   Ⓒ rushmore in South Dakota.
   Ⓓ none

10. Ⓐ Jeanne Goodwin, my cousin,
    Ⓑ is the President of the
    Ⓒ high school Latin Club.
    Ⓓ none

11. Ⓐ Jefferson City is the
    Ⓑ state Capital of the
    Ⓒ "Show-Me" state—Missouri.
    Ⓓ none

12. Ⓐ Christopher Columbus, an
    Ⓑ italian, discovered
    Ⓒ America for Spain.
    Ⓓ none

Columbus.

13. Ⓐ Patrick Henry, the great
    Ⓑ American patriot, said, "give
    Ⓒ me liberty or give me death."
    Ⓓ none

14. Ⓐ King Philip, chief of the
    Ⓑ Wampanoago, led the indians
    Ⓒ in a war against the New England Confederation.
    Ⓓ none

Name: _____ Date: _____

Unit 5 Test 2: *Punctuation*

Directions: Darken the circle next to the line containing an error in punctuation. Darken "D" if no error exists.

1. Ⓐ Well, I just met
   Ⓑ Mrs. Lucas our new
   Ⓒ school nurse from New York.
   Ⓓ none

2. Ⓐ On July 15, 1996,
   Ⓑ I visited my aunt
   Ⓒ in Anderson, Indiana.
   Ⓓ none

3. Ⓐ Orville Wright made
   Ⓑ his first plane flight
   Ⓒ on January 12, 1908.
   Ⓓ none

4. Ⓐ Mrs. Jenkins my neighbor
   Ⓑ works for the American
   Ⓒ Red Cross each Monday.
   Ⓓ none

5. Ⓐ My brother Aaron has recently
   Ⓑ finished reading The Challenge
   Ⓒ of the Sea a novel by Arthur C. Clarke.
   Ⓓ none

6. Ⓐ In Virginia, the great patriot
   Ⓑ Patrick Henry; fought against
   Ⓒ the passing of the Constitution.
   Ⓓ none

7. Ⓐ Quickly Mary washed the dishes,
   Ⓑ dried them, and put them
   Ⓒ on the shelves, she had just cleaned.
   Ⓓ none

101

Name: _____ Date: _____

Unit 5 Test 2: *Punctuation (Continued)*

8. Ⓐ Yes if Toby goes with you,
   Ⓑ you mustn't be out too
   Ⓒ late; he has a game tomorrow.
   Ⓓ none

9. Ⓐ When you finish your homework,
   Ⓑ Richard, please help me
   Ⓒ move the Smiths' piano.
   Ⓓ none

10. Ⓐ I've completed all my
    Ⓑ homework in history
    Ⓒ geography, English, and art.
    Ⓓ none

11. Ⓐ Trent, at this time of year,
    Ⓑ as you know, students visit
    Ⓒ the library to do they're research.
    Ⓓ none

12. Ⓐ Mrs. Arnold's appearance
    Ⓑ at the dance wasn't, of
    Ⓒ course, a shock to any of us.
    Ⓓ none

13. Ⓐ The following students have
    Ⓑ been awarded medals: Ann,
    Ⓒ Linda, Luanne, and Ginger
    Ⓓ none

14. Ⓐ The 7:50 train to
    Ⓑ Detroit, Michigan has
    Ⓒ been canceled, so I've heard.
    Ⓓ none.

15. Ⓐ Cora Davenport, our
    Ⓑ chemistry teacher, graduated
    Ⓒ from Texas Tech University.
    Ⓓ none

Name: _____ Date: _____

Creative Writing Application: *Nouns*

Directions: Write a paper using one of the prompts below. Use your best organizing skills. Brainstorm ideas, organize your thoughts, and plan your paper so that it does *all* and *only* what the prompt asks of you. Use correct grammar, appropriate word choices, vivid modifiers and phrases, and exciting verbs to make the reader actually see what you are saying. Proofread for errors in capitalization and punctuation.

Prompt 1:

Write a paper about all the things that make you feel safe. These could be people, places, or things. Mention them in some logical order. Give descriptions where needed. Explain any details that the reader would need to know to understand your point. Try to use plural nouns, possessive nouns, and at least one appositive.

Prompt 2:

You are in charge of designing a "treasure hunt" for your class. Decide how many teams to have and where the groups can go to get their items. Explain in detail what each group is required to do or get on the hunt. Use singular and plural nouns and singular and plural possessive nouns.

Name: _____   Date: _____

Creative Writing Application: *Pronouns*

Directions: Write a paper using one of the prompts below. Use your best organizing skills. Brainstorm ideas, organize your thoughts, and plan your paper so that it does *all* and *only* what the prompt asks of you. Use correct grammar, appropriate word choices, vivid modifiers and phrases, and exciting verbs to make the reader actually see what you are saying. Proofread for errors in capitalization and punctuation.

Prompt 1:

Write a letter to a friend or relative about a group project that you were involved with at school. Explain the project, but also tell who else was involved and their parts in the project. Use one or more pronouns in compound subjects and compound objects. Use pronouns in any situation, but make sure you have first established the antecedent.

Prompt 2:

Pretend you are a newspaper reporter on the scene of a serious accident or crime. You are interviewing witnesses to the incident. Use the five-question approach to the investigation—**who**, **what**, **where**, **how**, and **when**. Ask questions of the witnesses. Use **who**, **whom**, and **whose** in the questions you ask.

Name: _____   Date: _____

Creative Writing Application: *Adjectives*

Directions: Write a paper using one of the prompts below. Use your best organizing skills. Brainstorm ideas, organize your thoughts, and plan your paper so that it does *all* and *only* what the prompt asks of you. Use correct grammar, appropriate word choices, vivid modifiers and phrases, and exciting verbs to make the reader actually see what you are saying. Proofread for errors in capitalization and punctuation.

Prompt 1:

Consider one single thing about your school that you would like to see changed. Write a paper that tells what the problem or situation is and how you would like to see it changed. Use vivid adjectives that describe or modify and that paint a picture in words that you want your reader to "see." Defend your opinion with facts and examples that will sway the reader to see it your way.

Prompt 2:

Suppose you could be on any TV game show. What show would that be, and why? What would you like to win? What would be your strengths in performing on this show? Use adjectives and predicate adjectives to express your feelings and describe your thoughts.

Name: _____ Date: _____

Creative Writing Application: *Verbs*

Directions: Write a paper using one of the prompts below. Use your best organizing skills. Brainstorm ideas, organize your thoughts, and plan your paper so that it does *all* and *only* what the prompt asks of you. Use correct grammar, appropriate word choices, vivid modifiers and phrases, and exciting verbs to make the reader actually see what you are saying. Proofread for errors in capitalization and punctuation.

Prompt 1:

What effects do cigarette and alcohol advertising have on young people? You might want to interview some of your peers and some adults to find out what they believe to be the impact of such advertising. Then gather your information and organize your thoughts. Write a paper that strongly supports your topic sentence. Use examples and illustrations, as well as vivid verbs, to create an image in the reader's mind. Try to use transitive verbs, intransitive verbs, linking verbs, and helping verbs. In addition, use compound verbs where possible.

Prompt 2:

How is junior high or middle school different from elementary school? Write a paper that shares your thoughts about those differences. What are they? Are they all positive? Are some negative? How do they affect you? Organize your points carefully. You might group them and then discuss them. Concentrate on using different verb tenses.

Name: _____ Date: _____

Creative Writing Application: *Adverbs*

Directions: Write a paper using one of the prompts below. Use your best organizing skills. Brainstorm ideas, organize your thoughts, and plan your paper so that it does *all* and *only* what the prompt asks of you. Use correct grammar, appropriate word choices, vivid modifiers and phrases, and exciting verbs to make the reader actually see what you are saying. Proofread for errors in capitalization and punctuation.

Prompt 1:

Interview someone in your family, preferably a parent, grandparent, older aunt, or uncle. Ask them to share a story that happened long before you were born. Find out all the details and the correct order of events. Write a paper relating the story in an exciting way. Use vivid adverbs, including comparative and superlative forms.

Prompt 2:

Pretend you are very famous. For what are you famous? What have you achieved? What special skills do you have? What is your next goal in life? Write your paper using adverbs and adverb phrases that add life and description to your writing. You might try comparative and superlative forms of adverbs, too.

Name: _____   Date: _____

Creative Writing Application: *Prepositional Phrases*

Directions: Write a paper using one of the prompts below. Use your best organizing skills. Brainstorm ideas, organize your thoughts, and plan your paper so that it does *all* and *only* what the prompt asks of you. Use correct grammar, appropriate word choices, vivid modifiers and phrases, and exciting verbs to make the reader actually see what you are saying. Proofread for errors in capitalization and punctuation.

Prompt 1:

Suppose you were a store owner. Tell your plan to discourage people from stealing from you. What would you have in place? Think of at least three things that you feel would work. Be specific in describing and explaining each one. Tell how each would indeed discourage would-be thieves. Use adjective and adverb prepositional phrases in your paper.

Prompt 2:

If you could win any kind of trophy, what would it be? Write a paper explaining what the trophy represents and what it takes to win it. Then tell how you won the trophy. What were your accomplishments? Who were your biggest competitors? What does winning this trophy mean to your future? Use prepositional phrases to enhance your descriptions.

Name: _____   Date: _____

Creative Writing Application: *Sentences*

Directions: Write a paper using one of the prompts below. Use your best organizing skills. Brainstorm ideas, organize your thoughts, and plan your paper so that it does *all* and *only* what the prompt asks of you. Use correct grammar, appropriate word choices, vivid modifiers and phrases, and exciting verbs to make the reader actually see what you are saying. Proofread for errors in capitalization and punctuation.

Prompt 1:

Write about an incident that happened in elementary school. Who was involved? Was it humorous, or serious? What took place? How were you affected? How did you feel? Use compound subjects, compound predicates, and compound sentences.

Prompt 2:

Write a paper that explains some of the rules you have to follow at home. Try a "least to most important" order. What are the rules? Are there consequences for not following them? Describe in detail any rules that might be unique to your house or that some people may not understand. Use a variety of sentence types and lengths. Proofread for fragments and run-on sentences.

Name: _____ Date: _____

Creative Writing Application: *Language Skills*

Directions: Write a paper using one of the prompts below. Use your best organizing skills. Brainstorm ideas, organize your thoughts, and plan your paper so that it does *all* and *only* what the prompt asks of you. Use correct grammar, appropriate word choices, vivid modifiers and phrases, and exciting verbs to make the reader actually see what you are saying. Proofread for errors in capitalization and punctuation.

Prompt 1:

Pretend your best friend has told of his/her plan to run away from home, from school, from everything. What would you do and say to keep your friend from making a big mistake in life? Use correct subject-verb agreement and correct negatives. Avoid double negatives, however.

Prompt 2:

Imagine that you are running for class president. Write a speech outlining what you will do as president and what issues you will discuss during the campaign. Concentrate on good grammar, strong word choice, and sentence variety.

Name: _____ Date: _____

Creative Writing Application: *Capitalization and Punctuation*

Directions: Write a paper using one of the prompts below. Use your best organizing skills. Brainstorm ideas, organize your thoughts, and plan your paper so that it does *all* and *only* what the prompt asks of you. Use correct grammar, appropriate word choices, vivid modifiers and phrases, and exciting verbs to make the reader actually see what you are saying. Proofread for errors in capitalization and punctuation.

Prompt 1:

What will the world be like in the year 2030? What will schools be like? Will transportation change? Will we as Americans still be concerned with pollution and animal safety? What will happen to athletics at all levels? What might be your concerns as parents of children during this time? Use the best words for the assignment, and use sentence and tense variation.

Prompt 2:

Find the names, addresses, and birth dates of ten people in your room. Make a list of those names, addresses, and birthdays. Make sure you have used correct capitalization and punctuation.

Prompt 3:

What would a day be like at your school if there were no rules? What kinds of things would happen? How would the building climate be affected? How do you think you would feel?

Prompt 4:

Imagine that you need cash quickly. You decide to sell a favorite item with a newspaper advertisement. Write the advertisement, keeping in mind that creativity sells today. Use abbreviations, dates, times, and so on, correctly. What is the favorite item? How does it work, and what does it do?

Glossary of Terms

Abstract Noun: A quality, action, or idea

Action Verb: A verb that shows what a subject does, did, or will do

Adjective: A word that describes a noun and tells "what kind" or "how many"

Adverb: A word that describes a verb and tells "how," "where," or "when"

Agreement: Subjects and verbs must agree in tense and in number

Article: An adjective used to refer to a person, place, or thing ("a," "an," and "the")

Capitalization: Using an uppercase letter at the beginning of a word

Clause: A group of related words containing a subject and verb

Colon: (:) A mark of punctuation used to introduce a list of items

Comma: (,) A punctuation mark that separates words

Common Noun: A noun that names any person, place, or thing

Complete Predicate: The verb and all words that go with the verb

Complete Subject: Words containing the subject and all words in the subject

Compound Predicate: Two or more predicates joined by a conjunction

Compound Sentence: Two or more sentences joined by a comma and a conjunction

Compound Subject: Two or more subjects joined by a conjunction

Concrete Noun: A noun perceived by the senses

Conjunction: A part of speech that connects words or groups of words

Coordinating Conjunction: Used to connect two ideas of relatively equal importance

Correlative Conjunction: Shows contrast between two ideas

Contraction: Two words made into one word, using an apostrophe to indicate that some letters have been left out

Dangling Modifier: Words or phrases that appear at the beginning of sentences but fail to modify anything

Declarative Sentence: A sentence that tells something; a statement

Demonstrative Adjective: An adjective that tells "which one" ("this," "that," "these," "those")

Dependent Clause: A clause that does not express a complete thought

Direct Object: A noun or pronoun in the predicate that receives the verb action

Exclamatory Sentence: A sentence that shows strong feeling

112

Glossary of Terms

Fragment: A phrase that does not express a complete thought

Helping Verb: A verb that works with the main verb to make a verb phrase

Imperative Sentence: A sentence that gives an order

Indefinite Pronoun: A pronoun without an antecedent

Independent Clause: A clause that has a completed idea and can stand alone

Intensive Pronoun: A pronoun that adds emphasis to a noun or pronoun previously named

Interrogative Pronoun: A pronoun that introduces an interrogative sentence

Interrogative Sentence: A sentence that asks a question

Intransitive Verb: A verb that does not require a direct object

Irregular Verb: A verb that has a special form for the past tense

Linking Verb: A verb that tells who someone is or how he or she feels

Metaphor: A direct comparison between two unlike things without using the words "like" or "as"

Misplaced Modifier: Modifier that, because of location, modifies the wrong word

Negative: A word that means "no" or "not"

Object of a Preposition: A noun or pronoun that follows a preposition

Object Pronoun: Replaces a noun used as an object

Paragraph: A group of sentences related to a single topic

Personal Pronoun: A pronoun that takes the place of one or more nouns

Plural Noun: More than one person, place, thing, or idea

Possessive Noun: A noun that shows ownership

Possessive Pronoun: A pronoun that explains who or what owns something

Predicate: A verb that tells what the subject does

Predicate Adjective: An adjective that follows a linking verb and renames the subject

Predicate Noun: A noun in the sentence that follows a linking verb and renames the subject

Prefix: Letters placed at the beginning of a word to change its meaning

Preposition: A word that shows relationships between other words

Prepositional Phrase: A phrase that contains a preposition, an object, and any words in between

Glossary of Terms

Pronoun: A word that replaces a noun or another pronoun

Proper Adjective: An adjective made from a proper noun; a proper adjective is always capitalized

Proper Noun: A noun that names a special person, place, or thing; a proper noun is always capitalized

Quotation Marks: (" ") A pair of punctuation marks surrounding a quote to indicate a speaker

Reflexive Pronoun: A pronoun that reflects the action of the verb back to the subject

Run-on Sentence: Two or more sentences that run together without the proper punctuation or conjunctions

Semicolon: (;) Mark of punctuation that separates the clauses of a compound sentence when they are not joined by a coordinating conjunction

Sentence: A group of words that expresses a complete thought and contains a subject and a predicate

Simile: A comparison of two unlike things using the words "like" or "as"

Simple Predicate: Most important word in the complete predicate; the verb

Simple Subject: Most important word in the complete subject; the subject noun or pronoun

Subject: The word that tells what the sentence is about; a noun or pronoun

Subordinating Conjunction: Used to show the connection between a dependent clause and the rest of the sentence.

Suffix: Letters placed at the end of a word to change the meaning

Transitive Verb: An action verb that requires a direct object

Verb: Word that expresses action in a sentence

Verb Phrase: A group of words made up of a main verb and helping verb(s)

Grammar and Writing Skills: Grade 7+ Unit 1: Kinds of Nouns

Name: Date:

Unit 1: Kinds of Nouns

Tip

A **proper noun** names a particular person, place, idea, or thing. **Proper nouns** begin with a capital letter. All other **nouns** are **common nouns**.

Practice

Directions: Underline all nouns in the following sentences. Circle any letters that should be capitalized.

1. Kayla, give that book to your teacher, please.
2. atlanta and detroit are cities I would like to visit.
3. washington, d.c., is the capital of the united states.
4. The team will play football in the new stadium on Friday.
5. In what year was abraham lincoln elected president?
6. The title of the book is atlas gamer.

Tip

A **concrete noun** names something that is felt with the senses. An **abstract noun** names a quality, idea, or state of mind.

Example:
The tourists at Disney World wait with anticipation.
(concrete) (concrete) (abstract)

Practice

Directions: Put the nouns on the left in the correct column below.

	Concrete Nouns	Abstract Nouns
wind	1. wind	1. joy
joy		
pride		
cotton	2. cotton	2. pride
chocolate		
music	3. chocolate	3. anger
anger		
forgiveness	4. music	4. forgiveness

© Mark Twain Media, Inc., Publishers 2

Grammar and Writing Skills: Grade 7+ Unit 1: Using Nouns

Name: Date:

Unit 1: Using Nouns

Practice

Directions: Complete each sentence with an appropriate noun. Write what kind of noun it is on the line: **proper**, **concrete**, or **abstract**.

Example: *John laughed when he heard the story.* concrete

1. Max gave the permission slip to his answers will vary
2. My family went to ______ for our vacation. ______
3. Lynn was full of ______ as she watched the movie. ______
4. My favorite food is ______. ______
5. ______ is my next-door neighbor. ______
6. Miguel's brother borrowed his ______ yesterday. ______
7. It takes ______ to compete in a decathlon. ______
8. Last night we played ______ at the party. ______

Tip

Form the plural of most **nouns** by adding "s." *car - cars*
To **nouns** ending with a vowel and "y," add "s." *toy - toys*
To **nouns** ending with a consonant and "y," change the "y" to "i" and add "es." *spy - spies*

Practice

Directions: Change the following phrases to plural nouns.

1. that boy those boys
2. any person any persons
3. a solo solos
4. this culture those cultures

© Mark Twain Media, Inc., Publishers 3

Grammar and Writing Skills: Grade 7+ Unit 1: Possessive Nouns

Name: Date:

Unit 1: Possessive Nouns

Tip

Form the possessive of a **plural noun** ending in "**s**" by adding only an apostrophe ('). For **singular** or **plural nouns** not ending in "**s**," show possession by adding an apostrophe and an "**s.**" ('**s**).

Examples:
Singular *Anna's boots are new.*
Plural *The men's clinic opened recently.*
Plural *Lions' manes are often full and fluffy.*

Practice

Directions: Change these nouns to singular possessive, plural, and plural possessive.

Singular	Singular Possessive	Plural	Plural Possessive
1. army	army's	armies	armies'
2. judge	judge's	judges	judges'
3. tooth	tooth's	teeth	teeth's
4. story	story's	stories	stories'
5. knife	knife's	knives	knives'

Directions: Choose the correct noun to complete the phrase and write the correct possessive form of it in the blank.

horse house honey club secretary brush alto teacher

1. (plural) brushes' sharp bristles
2. (singular) alto's beautiful voice
3. (singular) honey's sweet taste
4. (singular) horse's shiny coat
5. (plural) secretaries' new computers
6. (plural) houses' fresh paint
7. (singular) teacher's favorite class

© Mark Twain Media, Inc., Publishers 4

Grammar and Writing Skills: Grade 7+ Unit 1: Plural Nouns Crossword

Name: Date:

Unit 1: Plural Nouns Crossword

Directions: Write the plural of each noun listed below in the corresponding box in the puzzle.

ACROSS	DOWN
2. puppy	1. deer
4. porch	3. swamp
7. radio	5. class
8. potato	6. country
12. goose	9. self
13. leaf	10. half
14. ox	11. man
16. mouse	15. trout
19. monkey	17. fox
20. thief	18. sky

© Mark Twain Media, Inc., Publishers 5

Grammar and Writing Skills: Grade 7+ Unit 1: Subject, Object, Personal, & Possessive Pronouns

Name: Date:

Unit 1: Subject & Object Pronouns, Personal & Possessive Pronouns

Practice

Directions: Read the descriptions below about each type of pronoun. Underline all the pronouns in each sentence. Then, under each description, find the pronouns of that type in the sentences and write them on the lines.

Personal pronouns take the place of one or more **nouns**.

1. We enjoyed the game last night.
2. Thanks for asking us to attend.
3. They played very well.

We us They

Subject pronouns are used as the **subject** of a **sentence**.

1. She borrowed my jacket for the party.
2. We will be happy when our friends arrive.
3. I always like to dance with you.

She We I

Object pronouns can be used as a **direct object**, **indirect object**, or an **object of a preposition**.

1. Mia showed me the photos from her vacation.
2. She told her friends that she bought souvenirs for them.
3. They were grateful and remembered to thank her.

me them her

Possessive pronouns are personal **pronouns** that show possession or ownership.

1. Jackie introduced her father to the class.
2. He told us about the job as mayor of our town.
3. Jackie's father is busier than mine.

her our mine

© Mark Twain Media, Inc., Publishers 6

Grammar and Writing Skills: Grade 7+ Unit 1: Other Types of Pronouns

Name: Date:

Unit 1: Other Types of Pronouns

Tip

An **interrogative pronoun** introduces an interrogative sentence.

Examples: *Who owns the car?*
Whom did you call?

(Note: Be careful to use "who" as the **subject** of a **sentence** and "whom" as the **object**.)

A **reflexive pronoun** reflects the action of the **verb** back to the **subject**.

Example: *I introduced myself to the new student.*

An **intensive pronoun** adds emphasis to a **noun** or **pronoun** just named.

Example: *The woman herself has not yet been told.*

An **indefinite pronoun** may refer to a **noun** but does not indicate a specific person, place, or thing.

Example: *Someone caught the foul ball.*

Practice

Directions: Underline the pronoun in each sentence and write what type of pronoun it is.

1. Most of the people heard the alarm. indefinite
2. Napoleon declared himself the emperor of France. reflexive
3. What is the answer to question three? interrogative
4. Anyone can obtain a library card. indefinite
5. The players themselves don't know the score. intensive
6. Which of the puppies belongs to Sierra? interrogative
7. Deborah bought herself a snack in the cafeteria. reflexive
8. The canyon itself has never been explored. intensive

Writing Application

Directions: Write three sentences of your own on your own paper. Use at least one pronoun in each sentence.

© Mark Twain Media, Inc., Publishers 7

Grammar and Writing Skills: Grade 7+ Unit 1: Using Pronouns

Name: Date:

Unit 1: Using Pronouns

Practice

Directions: Complete each sentence by adding an appropriate interrogative, reflexive, intensive, possessive, or indefinite pronoun. Write what kind of pronoun you used on the line beside the sentence.

Answers

1. Jacob let Sarah play with will vary ball. possessive
2. ______ of the cakes did you bring? interrogative
3. Brevin pulled ______ onto the platform. reflexive
4. Madison told ______ to be here at 3:00. indefinite
5. ______ was voted class president this year? interrogative
6. ______ of the questions can be left blank. indefinite

Writing Application

1. Write a sentence using "himself" as a **reflexive pronoun**.
Answers will vary.
2. Write a sentence using "anyone" as an **indefinite pronoun**.
3. Write a sentence using "which" as an **interrogative pronoun**.
4. Write a sentence using "you" as an **object pronoun**.
5. Write a sentence using "our" as a **possessive pronoun**.
6. Write a sentence using "they" as a **subject pronoun**.

© Mark Twain Media, Inc., Publishers 8

Grammar and Writing Skills: Grade 7+ Unit 1: Adjectives/Demonstrative Adjectives

Name: Date:

Unit 1: Adjectives/Demonstrative Adjectives

Tip

An **adjective** describes a **noun** or **pronoun**. **Adjectives** usually come just before the **noun** or **pronoun**.

Practice

Directions: Underline all the adjectives in the sentences below.

1. Large groups of people camp at this beautiful lake over the long weekend.
2. Excited children rush to the sandy beach for a cool swim.
3. Two men are playing catch under the shady elm tree.
4. Interested observers watch the noisy speedboats rush by.
5. Many boats have daring skiers behind them, skidding across the rough waves.
6. Three peaceful fishermen sit in an anchored boat on the far side of the lake.

Tip

"This," "that," "these," and "those" are **demonstrative adjectives** that modify **nouns** by telling **which one** or **which ones**.

Examples: *This car is a convertible.*
That car across the street is a hatchback.

Practice

Directions: Circle the correct form of the adjective in parentheses.

1. (This, That) man over there is very tall.
2. (Those, That) shoes look too big for you.
3. (These, This) pair might be better.
4. (That, Those) dog looks vicious.

© Mark Twain Media, Inc., Publishers 9

Grammar and Writing Skills: Grade 7+ Unit 1: Comparing With Adjectives

Name: Date:

Unit 1: Comparing With Adjectives

Tip

Adjectives can be used to compare two or more **nouns**. The word endings "er" or "est" or special words such as "less," "least," "more," and "most" are added to show comparison.

Examples:

	Comparative	Superlative
angry	*angrier*	*angriest*
fun	*less fun*	*least fun*

Practice

Directions: Write a comparative and superlative form of each adjective.

	Comparative	Superlative
1. daring	more daring	most daring
2. skinny	skinnier	skinniest
3. active	more active	most active
4. small	smaller	smallest
5. easy	easier	easiest
6. slow	slower	slowest
7. quiet	quieter	quietest
8. dark	darker	darkest

Directions: Write the correct form of the adjective in parentheses. (Note: these are adjectives that have irregular comparison forms.)

1. Now that his arm has healed, Bo is feeling better (good)
2. I have many cats, but Julie has more of them. (many)
3. My answer is bad but it could be worse (bad)
4. They saved the best for last. (good)
5. I have less money now than I did yesterday. (little)

© Mark Twain Media, Inc., Publishers 10

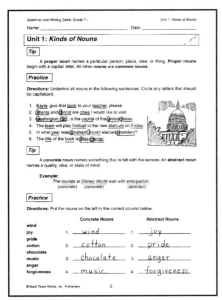

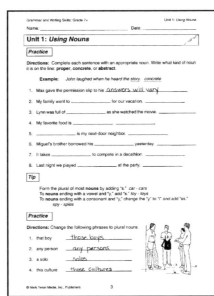

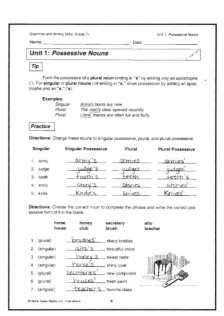

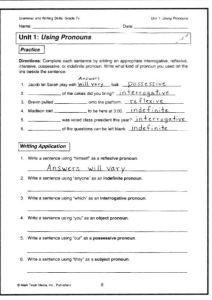

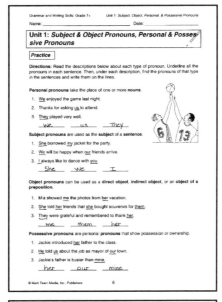

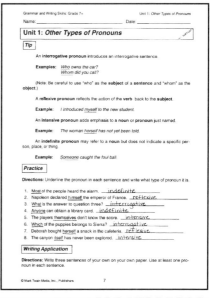

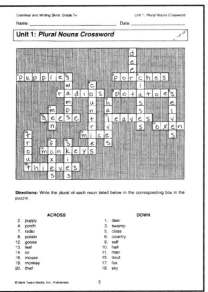

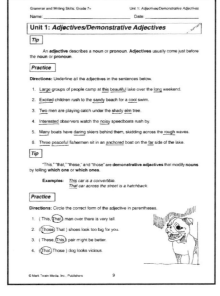

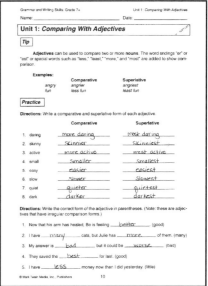

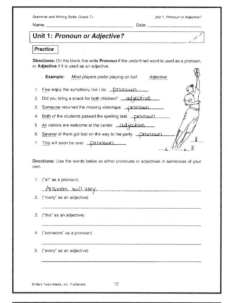

Grammar and Writing Skills: Grade 7+ — Unit 1: Pronoun or Adjective?

Name: ______ Date: ______

Unit 1: Pronoun or Adjective?

Practice

Directions: On the blank line write **Pronoun** if the underlined word is used as a pronoun, or **Adjective** if it is used as an adjective.

Example: *Most players prefer playing on turf.* *Adjective*

1. Few enjoy the symphony like I do. pronoun
2. Did you bring a snack for both children? adjective
3. Someone returned the missing videotape. pronoun
4. Both of the students passed the spelling test. pronoun
5. All visitors are welcome at the center. adjective
6. Several of them got lost on the way to the party. pronoun
7. This will soon be over. pronoun

Directions: Use the words below as either pronouns or adjectives in sentences of your own.

1. ("all" as a pronoun) Answers will vary.
2. ("many" as an adjective)
3. ("this" as an adjective)
4. ("someone" as a pronoun)
5. ("every" as an adjective)

© Mark Twain Media, Inc., Publishers 12

Grammar and Writing Skills: Grade 7+ — Unit 1: Principal Parts of Verbs

Name: ______ Date: ______

Unit 1: Principal Parts of Verbs

Tip

Every **verb** has four principal parts: the **present**, the **present participle**, the **past**, and the **past participle**.

Present	Present Participle	Past	Past Participle
look	looking	looked	(have) looked

Tip

Most **verbs** are regular and form their **past** and **past participles** by adding "d" or "ed." But some **verbs** are irregular and form their **past** and **past participles** differently.

Present	Present Participle	Past	Past Participle
begin	beginning	began	(have) begun
buy	buying	bought	(have) bought
forget	forgetting	forgot	(have) forgotten
grow	growing	grew	(have) grown
set	setting	set	(have) set

Practice

Directions: See how many of the following irregular verbs you already know. Complete the last three principal parts.

Present	Present Participle	Past	Past Participle
1. sit	sitting	sat	(have) sat
2. bite	biting	bit	(have) bitten
3. lie	lying	lied or lay	(have) lied or lain
4. go	going	went	(have) gone
5. burst	bursting	burst	(have) burst
6. ring	ringing	rang	(have) rung
7. sing	singing	sang	(have) sung
8. lose	losing	lost	(have) lost
9. blow	blowing	blew	(have) blown
10. raise	raising	raised	(have) raised
11. steal	stealing	stole	(have) stolen

© Mark Twain Media, Inc., Publishers 13

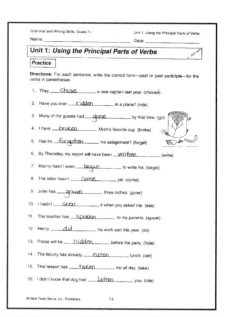

Grammar and Writing Skills: Grade 7+ — Unit 1: Using the Principal Parts of Verbs

Name: ______ Date: ______

Unit 1: Using the Principal Parts of Verbs

Practice

Directions: For each sentence, write the correct form—past or past participle—for the verbs in parentheses.

1. They chose a new captain last year. (choose)
2. Have you ever ridden in a plane? (ride)
3. Many of the guests had gone by that time. (go)
4. I have broken Mom's favorite cup. (broke)
5. Has he forgotten his assignment? (forget)
6. By Thursday, my report will have been written (write)
7. Manny hasn't even begun to write his. (begin)
8. The letter hasn't come yet. (come)
9. John has grown three inches. (grow)
10. I hadn't seen it when you asked me. (see)
11. The teacher has spoken to my parents. (speak)
12. Henry did his work well this year. (do)
13. Prizes will be hidden before the party. (hide)
14. The faculty has already eaten lunch. (eat)
15. That lesson has taken me all day. (take)
16. I didn't know that dog had bitten you. (bite)

© Mark Twain Media, Inc., Publishers 14

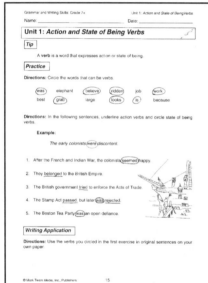

Grammar and Writing Skills: Grade 7+ — Unit 1: Action and State of Being Verbs

Name: ______ Date: ______

Unit 1: Action and State of Being Verbs

Tip

A **verb** is a word that expresses action or state of being.

Practice

Directions: Circle the words that can be verbs.

(was) elephant (believe) (ridden) job (work) best (grab) large (looks) (is) because

Directions: In the following sentences, underline action verbs and circle state of being verbs.

Example:

The early colonists (were) discontent.

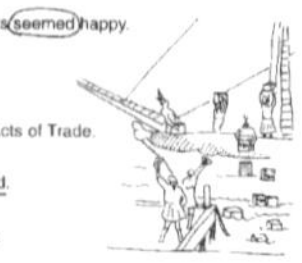

1. After the French and Indian War, the colonists (seemed) happy.
2. They belonged to the British Empire.
3. The British government tried to enforce the Acts of Trade.
4. The Stamp Act passed, but later (was) rejected.
5. The Boston Tea Party (was) an open defiance.

Writing Application

Directions: Use the verbs you circled in the first exercise in original sentences on your own paper.

© Mark Twain Media, Inc., Publishers 15

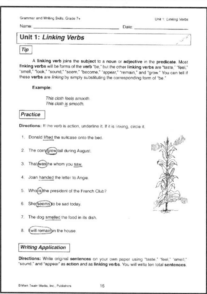

Grammar and Writing Skills: Grade 7+ — Unit 1: Linking Verbs

Name: ______ Date: ______

Unit 1: Linking Verbs

Tip

A **linking verb** joins the **subject** to a **noun** or **adjective** in the **predicate**. Most **linking verbs** will be forms of the **verb** "be," but the other **linking verbs** are "taste," "feel," "smell," "look," "sound," "seem," "become," "appear," "remain," and "grow." You can tell if these **verbs** are *linking* by simply substituting the corresponding form of "be."

Example:

This cloth feels smooth.
This cloth is smooth.

Practice

Directions: If the verb is action, underline it. If it is linking, circle it.

1. Donald lifted the suitcase onto the bed.
2. The corn (grew) tall during August.
3. That (was) he whom you saw.
4. Joan handed the letter to Angie.
5. Who (is) the president of the French Club?
6. She (seems) to be sad today.
7. The dog smelled the food in its dish.
8. I (will remain) in the house.

Writing Application

Directions: Write original **sentences** on your own paper using "taste," "feel," "smell," "sound," and "appear" as **action** and as **linking verbs**. You will write ten total **sentences**.

© Mark Twain Media, Inc., Publishers 16

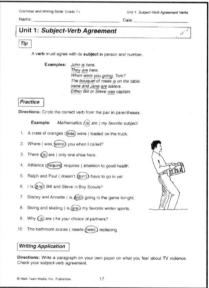

Grammar and Writing Skills: Grade 7+ — Unit 1: Subject-Verb Agreement Verbs

Name: ______ Date: ______

Unit 1: Subject-Verb Agreement

Tip

A **verb** must agree with its **subject** in person and number.

Examples: *John is here.*
They are here.
When were you going, Tom?
The bouquet of roses is on the table.
Irene and Jane are sisters.
Either Bill or Steve was captain.

Practice

Directions: Circle the correct verb from the pair in parentheses.

Example: *Mathematics ((is) are) my favorite subject.*

1. A crate of oranges ((was) were) loaded on the truck.
2. Where (was, (were)) you when I called?
3. There ((is) are) only one shoe here.
4. Athletics ((require) requires) attention to good health.
5. Ralph and Paul (doesn't, (don't)) have to go in yet.
6. (Is, (Are)) Bill and Steve in Boy Scouts?
7. Stacey and Annette (is, (are)) going to the game tonight.
8. Skiing and skating (is, (are)) my favorite winter sports.
9. Why ((is) are) he your choice of partners?
10. The bathroom scales (needs, (need)) replacing.

Writing Application

Directions: Write a paragraph on your own paper on what you feel about TV violence. Check your subject-verb agreement.

© Mark Twain Media, Inc., Publishers 17

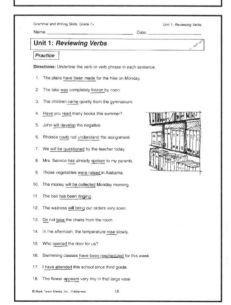

Grammar and Writing Skills: Grade 7+ — Unit 1: Reviewing Verbs

Name: ______ Date: ______

Unit 1: Reviewing Verbs

Practice

Directions: Underline the verb or verb phrase in each sentence.

1. The plans have been made for the hike on Monday.
2. The lake was completely frozen by noon.
3. The children came quietly from the gymnasium.
4. Have you read many books this summer?
5. John will develop the negative.
6. Rhonda could not understand the assignment.
7. We will be questioned by the teacher today.
8. Mrs. Service has already spoken to my parents.
9. Those vegetables were raised in Alabama.
10. The money will be collected Monday morning.
11. The bell has been ringing.
12. The waitress will bring our orders very soon.
13. Do not take the chairs from the room.
14. In the afternoon, the temperature rose slowly.
15. Who opened the door for us?
16. Swimming classes have been rescheduled for this week.
17. I have attended this school since third grade.
18. The flower appears very tiny in that large vase.

© Mark Twain Media, Inc., Publishers 18

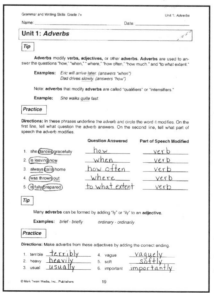

Grammar and Writing Skills: Grade 7+ — Unit 1: Adverbs

Name: ______ Date: ______

Unit 1: Adverbs

Tip

Adverbs modify **verbs, adjectives,** or other **adverbs. Adverbs** are used to answer the questions "how," "when," "where," "how often," "how much," and "to what extent."

Examples: *Eric will arrive later. (answers "when")*
Dad drives slowly. (answers "how")

Note: **adverbs** that modify **adverbs** are called "qualifiers" or "intensifiers."

Example: *She walks quite fast.*

Practice

Directions: In these phrases underline the adverb and circle the word it modifies. On the first line, tell what question the adverb answers. On the second line, tell what part of speech the adverb modifies.

	Question Answered	Part of Speech Modified
1. she (dances) gracefully	how	verb
2. (is leaving) now	when	verb
3. always (calls) home	how often	verb
4. (was thrown) out	where	verb
5. (is) fully (prepared)	to what extent	verb

Tip

Many **adverbs** can be formed by adding "ly" or "ily" to an **adjective**.

Examples: *brief - briefly* *ordinary - ordinarily*

Practice

Directions: Make adverbs from these adjectives by adding the correct ending.

1. terrible terribly
2. heavy heavily
3. usual usually
4. vague vaguely
5. soft softly
6. important importantly

© Mark Twain Media, Inc., Publishers 19

Grammar and Writing Skills: Grade 7+ — Unit 1: Adjectives and Adverbs

Name: ______ Date: ______

Unit 1: Adjectives and Adverbs

Tip

Adverbs generally answer "how," "when," "where," "how often," and "how much." **Adjectives** answer "what kind," "which one," and "how many."

Practice

Directions: Cross out the word that is not correct. Write **Adj.** or **Adv.** above the correct word.

1. This form must be completed (~~accurate~~, accurately). adv.
2. Your shirt looks (sloppy, ~~sloppily~~). adj.
3. You can dress (~~sloppy~~, sloppily) on the weekend. adv.
4. The kittens were (warm, ~~warmly~~) under the blanket. adj.
5. Tina plays softball (~~skillful~~, skillfully). adv.
6. The train ride to San Francisco was (slow, ~~slowly~~). adj.
7. The horse plodded (~~heavy~~, heavily) down the trail. adv.
8. My street is (smooth, ~~smoothly~~) enough for skateboarding. adj.

Directions: Circle the adjectives and underline the adverbs.

1. The (lively) puppy trotted quickly to the door.
2. When the (little) boy opened the door, the puppy ran outside.
3. (Two) (chattering) birds flew dangerously close to the dog's head.
4. The (playful) puppy barked loudly at the birds as they flew away.
5. Then he grew (tired) and came inside to rest.
6. The (sleepy) puppy was soon curled cozily in front of the (warm) fireplace.

© Mark Twain Media, Inc., Publishers 21

Unit 1: Modifiers

Practice

Directions: Label the underlined modifiers in each sentence. Write "A" over adjectives, "NM" over noun modifiers (nouns used as adjectives), or "VM" over verb modifiers (verbs used as adjectives).

Example:
    A   NM
Our favorite family doctor moved away.

1. The large, sliding avalanche was a danger to skiers. (A, VM)
2. He painted a sad, drooping face on the clown. (A, VM)
3. The drizzling rain ruined our cardboard clubhouse. (VM, NM)
4. The generous church donation allowed the group to visit Central America. (A, NM)
5. The successful running back set our school record. (A, VM)
6. My hospital bill was costly. (NM)
7. The purple blooming flowers attracted bumble bees. (A, VM)
8. The plastic and glass necklace looked real. (NM, NM)
9. The blaring fire alarm started everyone. (VM, NM)
10. A green swimming turtle moved smoothly through the water. (A, VM)

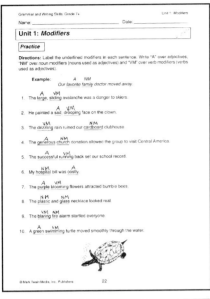

Unit 1: Direct Objects

Tip

A **direct object** is a word that tells who or what receives the action of the **verb**.
Example: Annette adjusted the volume on the radio. (answers "what")

In some sentences, the **direct object** is compound.
Example: Grandmother gave money and clothes to the charity. (answers "what")

Practice

Directions: Underline the verb and circle the direct object in each sentence.

1. Mimi called Mr. Robbins last night.
2. The actor memorized his lines for the play.
3. The nurse checked my pulse.
4. The club elected Scott as treasurer.
5. James wrote a poem for English homework.
6. Sharon lost her best earrings.
7. Many people read the newspaper daily.
8. The store lost business after the fire.
9. I invited Manny to the dance.
10. That photographer takes beautiful pictures.
11. Melinda visited China last year.
12. Brandi collects foreign stamps.
13. I make my bed every morning.
14. I wore Jen's dress to the dance.
15. Ben asked me to join his team.

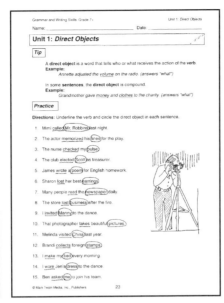

Unit 1: Indirect Objects

Tip

An **indirect object** is a noun or pronoun that tells "to whom" or "for whom" the action of the **verb** is done.

Example: Ms. Nelson told us a funny story.
       S   V   I.O.   D.O.

Practice

Directions: Label the subject (S), verb (V), direct object (D.O.), and indirect object (I.O.) in each sentence.

Example: S   V   I.O.   D.O.
The teacher handed Joe his assignment.

1. The bird provides her babies worms to eat. (S V IO DO)
2. My uncle taught me fishing techniques. (S V IO DO)
3. The group made their sponsor thank-you cards. (S V IO DO)
4. Leslie showed her boss the new blueprints. (S V IO DO)
5. The reporter read us his latest column. (S V IO DO)
6. Our teacher left the substitute the answer key. (S V IO DO)
7. The scientist gave the world a cure for the disease. (S V IO DO)
8. Someone showed me the right road to take. (S V IO DO)
9. You sent Nate a long e-mail. (S V IO DO)
10. Simon told her the correct address. (S V IO DO)

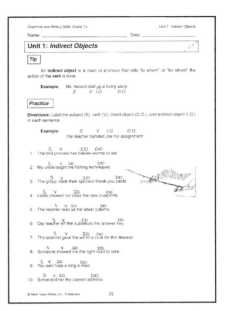

Unit 1: Conjunctions

Tip

A **coordinating conjunction** is used to connect two ideas of relatively equal importance.
Example: Did they take a boat or a plane?

Coordinating Conjunctions
and   but   or
for   nor   yet

A **subordinating conjunction** is used to show the connection between a **dependent clause** and the rest of the sentence.
Example: We will leave when Sam arrives.

Subordinating Conjunctions
if   until   although
as   when   because
since   unless   before

A **correlative conjunction** is used to show contrast between two ideas.
Example: The tree is either a maple or an oak.

Correlative Conjunctions
not only. . . but also   either. . . or
whether. . . if   neither. . . nor

Practice

Directions: Underline the conjunction in each sentence. On the line write **coordinating**, **subordinating**, or **correlative** to indicate how the conjunction is used.

1. Neither Alan nor I had done our homework. Correlative
2. The picnic will be tomorrow unless it rains. Subordinating
3. In the summer I like to fish and swim. Coordinating
4. John will lose the race unless he hurries. Subordinating
5. They invited us, but we forgot to attend. Coordinating
6. Trish won the award, for she had worked the hardest. Coordinating

Unit 1: Using Conjunctions

Practice

Directions: Write an appropriate conjunction to complete each sentence.

1. Dad got promoted when he did that extra project.
2. Haven't you either visited Gary or called him?
3. It may sound funny, but the album is very good.
4. Dolphins not only communicate, but also learn.
5. Your horse can go over the bridge and walk through the creek.
6. If it snows, the trip will be canceled.
7. The freshman class and the junior high built the float together.
8. I can't come over unless an adult is present.

Directions: Combine the sentences below using a subordinating conjunction from the box. Use a different subordinating conjunction each time.

| because | if | after |
| whenever | until | before |

1. We plan to ride our bikes. It rains.
Answers will vary.
2. You can stay home. You are concerned about lightning.
3. Maybe we should all wait. The rain stops.
4. Chances for an accident increase. The road is slippery.
5. I must remember to wear my helmet. I have fallen before.

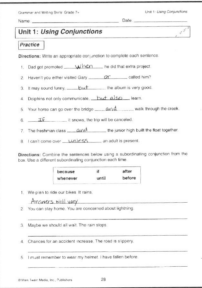

Unit 1: Prepositions

Tip

A **preposition** shows a relationship between a **noun** or **pronoun** (the object) and another word in the **sentence**.

Example: prep.   obj.
He threw the ball through the goal.

Practice

Directions: Write an object for each preposition.

1. upon   Answers will vary.
2. from
3. above
4. to
5. beside
6. in
7. under
8. near
9. on

Directions: Circle the preposition in each sentence and underline the object of the preposition.

Example: I dropped my keys into my purse.

1. On a summer day, people like to be outdoors.
2. A young girl swam toward the dock.
3. A wasp flew into the house.
4. Smoke from the grill filled the air.
5. The fisherman leaned against a rock while fishing.
6. Angel's flowered kite blew in the wind.
7. After school, the Johnson kids headed to the park.
8. Little children were climbing on the jungle gym.
9. Steve jumped off the diving board.
10. A squirrel scrambled up the nearest tree.

Unit 1: Prepositional Phrases

Tip

A **prepositional phrase** is a group of words that begins with a **preposition** and ends with a **noun** or **pronoun**.
Example: Chicago is located near the lake.

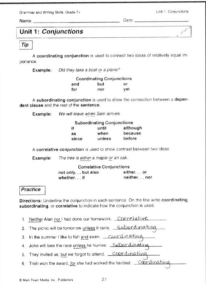

Practice

Directions: Underline the prepositional phrases in each sentence. Circle the objects of prepositions. The first one is done for you.

1. Corey went to the movie with Sara.
2. My cat drinks water from the kitchen sink.
3. The plane soared from the runway into the sky.
4. The school bus slowed to a halt at the railroad crossing.

Directions: Use each preposition in a sentence of your own. Put parentheses around the prepositional phrase.

1. above   Answers will vary.
2. up
3. against
4. on
5. beside
6. from
7. near
8. at

Unit 1: Prepositional Phrases as Adjectives and Adverbs

Tip

When a **prepositional phrase** modifies a **noun**, it acts as an **adjective**.
Example: The street to the right leads home. (phrase modifies "street")

When a **prepositional phrase** modifies a **verb**, it acts as an **adverb**.
Example: Today Martha left for the airport. (phrase modifies "left")

Practice

Directions: On the line after each sentence, write **ADJ** if the prepositional phrase functions as an adjective in the sentence, and write **ADV** if the prepositional phrase functions as an adverb.

1. My family went to the circus. ADV
2. The tent was pitched in a large field. ADV
3. I liked the tiger with the black stripes. ADJ
4. One brave man balanced himself on the high wire. ADV
5. The lady on horseback had grace and talent. ADJ
6. Several clowns climbed into a tiny car. ADV
7. The people beside the lion cage heard the roars. ADJ
8. Near the end the crowd gave the circus loud applause. ADV

Writing Application

Directions: Write five more sentences on your own paper describing what you might see, hear, or do at a circus. Use at least one prepositional phrase in each sentence.

Unit 1: Finding and Using Prepositional Phrases

Practice

Directions: Underline all the prepositional phrases in each sentence.

1. In a monarchy, the head of the country is a king or queen.
2. A democracy is any form of government that is elected by popular vote.
3. A nation with a dictator cannot have free elections.
4. Governments can make trade agreements with other countries.
5. The United Nations, an organization of many countries, meets in New York.
6. The United States of America has been an independent nation since 1776.
7. Across the ocean, Great Britain represents a long tradition of monarchy.

Writing Application

Directions: Pretend that you have gathered a group of people and pets for a photograph. Write five sentences describing how everyone should be positioned. Using the prepositions below, put a prepositional phrase in each sentence.

| beside | near | onto | from | behind |

Answers will vary.

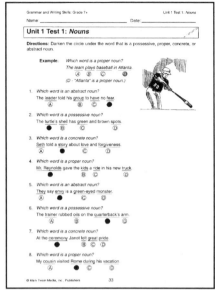

Unit 1 Test 1: *Nouns*

Directions: Darken the circle under the word that is a possessive, proper, concrete, or abstract noun.

Example: *Which word is a proper noun?*
The team plays baseball in Atlanta.
(D - "Atlanta" is a proper noun.)

1. Which word is an abstract noun?
2. Which word is a possessive noun?
3. Which word is a concrete noun?
4. Which word is a proper noun?
5. Which word is an abstract noun?
6. Which word is a possessive noun?
7. Which word is a concrete noun?
8. Which word is a proper noun?

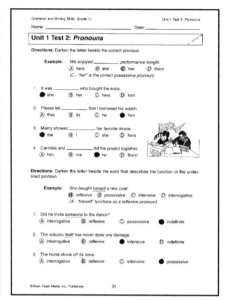

Unit 1 Test 2: *Pronouns*

Directions: Darken the letter beside the correct pronoun.

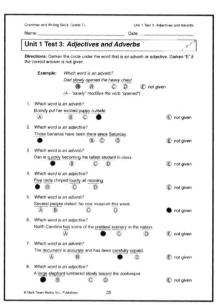

Unit 1 Test 3: *Adjectives and Adverbs*

Directions: Darken the circle under the word that is an adverb or adjective. Darken "E" if the correct answer is not given.

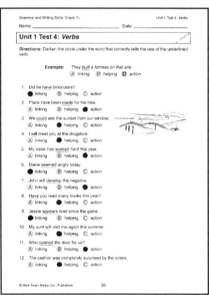

Unit 1 Test 4: *Verbs*

Directions: Darken the circle under the word that correctly tells the use of the underlined verb.

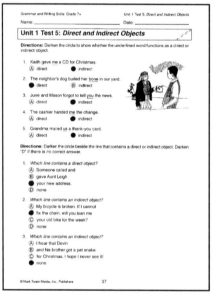

Unit 1 Test 5: *Direct and Indirect Objects*

Directions: Darken the circle to show whether the underlined word functions as a direct or indirect object.

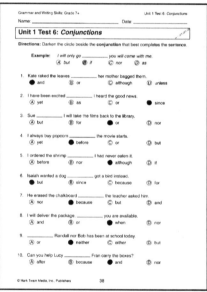

Unit 1 Test 6: *Conjunctions*

Directions: Darken the circle beside the **conjunction** that best completes the sentence.

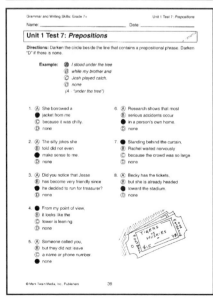

Unit 1 Test 7: *Prepositions*

Directions: Darken the circle beside the line that contains a prepositional phrase. Darken "D" if there is none.

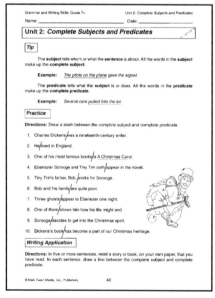

Unit 2: *Complete Subjects and Predicates*

Tip

The **subject** tells whom or what the **sentence** is about. All the words in the **subject** make up the **complete subject**.

The **predicate** tells what the **subject** is or does. All the words in the **predicate** make up the **complete predicate**.

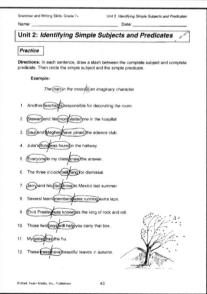

Unit 2: *Identifying Simple Subjects and Predicates*

Practice

Directions: In each sentence, draw a slash between the complete subject and complete predicate. Then circle the simple subject and the simple predicate.

Grammar and Writing Skills: Grade 7+ — Unit 2: Simple Sentences

Name: ______ Date: ______

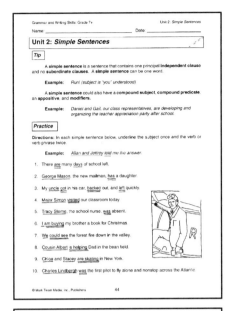

Unit 2: *Simple Sentences*

Tip

A **simple sentence** is a sentence that contains one principal **independent clause** and no **subordinate clauses**. A **simple sentence** can be one word.

Example: *Run! (subject is "you" understood)*

A **simple sentence** could also have a **compound subject, compound predicate**, an **appositive**, and **modifiers**.

Example: *Daniel and Gail, our class representatives, are developing and organizing the teacher appreciation party after school.*

Practice

Directions: In each simple sentence below, underline the subject once and the verb or verb phrase twice.

Example: *Allan and Jeffrey told me the answer.*

1. There are many days of school left.
2. George Mason, the new mailman, has a daughter.
3. My uncle got in his car, backed out, and left quickly.
4. Major Simon visited our classroom today.
5. Tracy Sterne, the school nurse, was absent.
6. I am buying my brother a book for Christmas.
7. We could see the forest fire down in the valley.
8. Cousin Albert is helping Dad in the bean field.
9. Chloe and Stacey are skating in New York.
10. Charles Lindbergh was the first pilot to fly alone and nonstop across the Atlantic.

© Mark Twain Media, Inc., Publishers 44

Grammar and Writing Skills: Grade 7+ — Unit 2: Compound Sentences

Name: ______ Date: ______

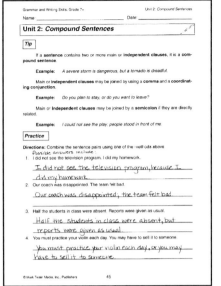

Unit 2: *Compound Sentences*

Tip

If a **sentence** contains two or more main or **independent clauses**, it is a **compound sentence**.

Example: *A severe storm is dangerous, but a tornado is dreadful.*

Main or **independent clauses** may be joined by using a **comma** and a **coordinating conjunction**.

Example: *Do you plan to stay, or do you want to leave?*

Main or **independent clauses** may be joined by a **semicolon** if they are directly related.

Example: *I could not see the play; people stood in front of me.*

Practice

Directions: Combine the sentence pairs using one of the methods above.

Possible answers include:

1. I did not see the television program. I did my homework.
   I did not see the television program, because I did my homework.
2. Our coach was disappointed. The team felt bad.
   Our coach was disappointed; the team felt bad.
3. Half the students in class were absent. Reports were given as usual.
   Half the students in class were absent, but reports were given as usual.
4. You must practice your violin each day. You may have to sell it to someone.
   You must practice your violin each day, or you may have to sell it to someone.

© Mark Twain Media, Inc., Publishers 45

Grammar and Writing Skills: Grade 7+ — Unit 2: Clauses

Name: ______ Date: ______

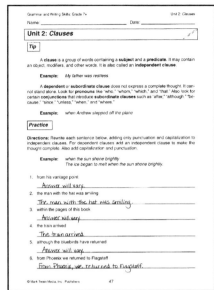

Unit 2: *Clauses*

Tip

A **clause** is a group of words containing a **subject** and a **predicate**. It may contain an object, modifiers, and other words. It is also called an **independent clause**.

Example: *My father was restless.*

A **dependent** or **subordinate clause** does not express a complete thought. It cannot stand alone. Look for **pronouns** like "who," "whom," "which," and "that." Also look for certain **conjunctions** that introduce **subordinate clauses** such as "after," "although," "because," "since," "unless," "when," and "where."

Example: *when Andrew stepped off the plane*

Practice

Directions: Rewrite each sentence below, adding only punctuation and capitalization to independent clauses. For dependent clauses add an independent clause to make the thought complete. Also add capitalization and punctuation.

Example: *when the sun shone brightly*
The ice began to melt when the sun shone brightly.

1. from his vantage point
   Answer will vary.
2. the man with the hat was smiling
   The man with the hat was smiling.
3. within the pages of this book
   Answer will vary.
4. the train arrived
   The train arrived.
5. although the bluebirds have returned
   Answer will vary.
6. from Phoenix we returned to Flagstaff
   From Phoenix, we returned to Flagstaff.

© Mark Twain Media, Inc., Publishers 47

Grammar and Writing Skills: Grade 7+ — Unit 2: Finding Dependent Clauses

Name: ______ Date: ______

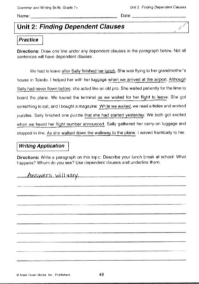

Unit 2: *Finding Dependent Clauses*

Practice

Directions: Draw one line under any dependent clauses in the paragraph below. Not all sentences will have dependent clauses.

We had to leave after Sally finished her lunch. She was flying to her grandmother's house in Toledo. I helped her with her luggage when we arrived at the airport. Although Sally had never flown before, she acted like an old pro. She waited patiently for the time to board the plane. We toured the terminal as we waited for her flight to leave. She got something to eat, and I bought a magazine. While we waited, we read articles and worked puzzles. Sally finished one puzzle that she had started yesterday. We both got excited when we heard her flight number announced. Sally gathered her carry-on luggage and stepped in line. As she walked down the walkway to the plane, I waved frantically to her.

Writing Application

Directions: Write a paragraph on this topic: Describe your lunch break at school. What happens? Whom do you see? Use dependent clauses and underline them.

Answers will vary.

© Mark Twain Media, Inc., Publishers 48

Grammar and Writing Skills: Grade 7+ — Unit 2: Finding Fragments

Name: ______ Date: ______

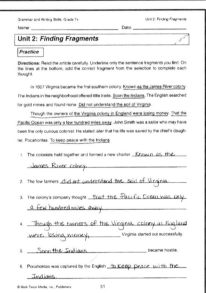

Unit 2: *Finding Fragments*

Practice

Directions: Read the article carefully. Underline only the sentence fragments you find. On the lines at the bottom, add the correct fragment from the selection to complete each thought.

In 1607 Virginia became the first southern colony. Known as the James River colony. The Indians in the neighborhood offered little trade. Soon the Indians. The English searched for gold mines and found none. Did not understand the soil of Virginia.

Though the owners of the Virginia colony in England were losing money. That the Pacific Ocean was only a few hundred miles away. John Smith was a sailor who may have been the only curious colonist. He stated later that his life was saved by the chief's daughter, Pocahontas. To keep peace with the Indians.

1. The colonists held together and formed a new charter Known as the James River colony.
2. The few farmers did not understand the soil of Virginia.
3. The colony's company thought that the Pacific Ocean was only a few hundred miles away.
4. Though the owners of the Virginia colony in England were losing money, Virginia started out successfully.
5. Soon the Indians became hostile.
6. Pocahontas was captured by the English to keep peace with the Indians.

© Mark Twain Media, Inc., Publishers 51

Grammar and Writing Skills: Grade 7+ — Unit 2: Correcting Fragments and Run-on Sentences

Name: ______ Date: ______

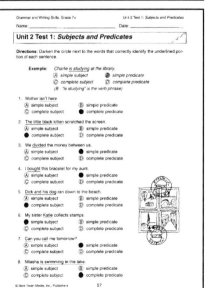

Unit 2: *Correcting Fragments and Run-on Sentences*

Practice

Directions: Read the sentences carefully. If you find no mistakes, write "correct" on the line. For fragments and run-on sentences, rewrite the sentence with proper corrections.

Possible answers include:

1. Brazil is full of natural wonders the Amazon River is just one.
   Brazil is full of natural wonders. The Amazon River is just one.
2. The Amazon River runs through the world's largest rain forest.
   Correct
3. Native Americans hunt and fish there their lives untouched by the modern world.
   Native Americans hunt and fish there, their lives untouched by the modern world.
4. Brazil has fertile soil. That produces coffee, cocoa, and sugar cane.
   Brazil has fertile soil that produces coffee, cocoa, and sugar cane.
5. The country has serious economic problems.
   Correct
6. The Amazon rain forest is being destroyed. To make new farmland and grazing land.
   The Amazon rain forest is being destroyed to make new farmland and grazing land.

Writing Application

Directions: Using your own paper, write on the following topic: What makes your best friend your best friend? Be specific and use complete sentences. Check for fragments and run-on sentences.

© Mark Twain Media, Inc., Publishers 53

Grammar and Writing Skills: Grade 7+ — Unit 2: Combining Sentences

Name: ______ Date: ______

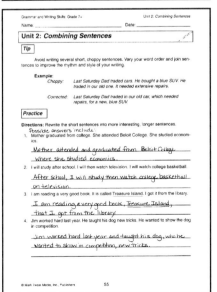

Unit 2: *Combining Sentences*

Tip

Avoid writing several short, choppy sentences. Vary your word order and join sentences to improve the rhythm and style of your writing.

Example:
Choppy: *Last Saturday Dad traded cars. He bought a blue SUV. He traded in our old one. It needed extensive repairs.*
Corrected: *Last Saturday Dad traded in our old car, which needed repairs, for a new, blue SUV.*

Practice

Directions: Rewrite the short sentences into more interesting, longer sentences.

Possible answers include:

1. Mother graduated from college. She attended Beloit College. She studied economics.
   Mother attended and graduated from Beloit College where she studied economics.
2. I will study after school. I will then watch television. I will watch college basketball.
   After school, I will study then watch college basketball on television.
3. I am reading a very good book. It is called Treasure Island. I got it from the library.
   I am reading a very good book, Treasure Island, that I got from the library.
4. Jim worked hard last year. He taught his dog new tricks. He wanted to show the dog in competition.
   Jim worked hard last year and taught his dog, who he wanted to show in competition, new tricks.

© Mark Twain Media, Inc., Publishers 55

Grammar and Writing Skills: Grade 7+ — Unit 2: Misplaced and Dangling Modifiers

Name: ______ Date: ______

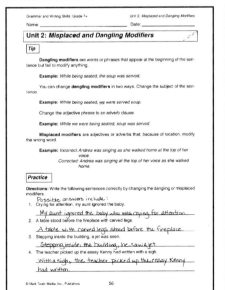

Unit 2: *Misplaced and Dangling Modifiers*

Tip

Dangling modifiers are words or phrases that appear at the beginning of the sentence but fail to modify anything.

Example: *While being seated, the soup was served.*

You can change **dangling modifiers** in two ways. Change the subject of the sentence.

Example: *While being seated, we were served soup.*

Change the adjective phrase to an adverb clause.

Example: *While we were being seated, soup was served.*

Misplaced modifiers are adjectives or adverbs that, because of location, modify the wrong word.

Example: *Incorrect: Andrea was singing as she walked home at the top of her voice.*
Corrected: Andrea was singing at the top of her voice as she walked home.

Practice

Directions: Write the following sentences correctly by changing the dangling or misplaced modifiers.

Possible answers include:

1. Crying for attention, my aunt ignored the baby.
   My aunt ignored the baby who was crying for attention.
2. A table stood before the fireplace with carved legs.
   A table with carved legs stood before the fireplace.
3. Stepping inside the building, a jet was seen.
   Stepping inside the building, he saw a jet.
4. The teacher picked up the essay Kenny had written with a sigh.
   With a sigh, the teacher picked up the essay Kenny had written.

© Mark Twain Media, Inc., Publishers 56

Grammar and Writing Skills: Grade 7+ — Unit 2 Test 1: Subjects and Predicates

Name: ______ Date: ______

Unit 2 Test 1: *Subjects and Predicates*

Directions: Darken the circle next to the words that correctly identify the underlined portion of each sentence.

Example: *Charlie is studying at the library.*
Ⓐ *simple subject* ● *simple predicate*
Ⓒ *complete subject* Ⓓ *complete predicate*
(B "is studying" is the verb phrase)

1. Mother isn't here.
   Ⓐ simple subject Ⓑ simple predicate
   Ⓒ complete subject ● complete predicate
2. The little black kitten scratched the screen.
   Ⓐ simple subject Ⓑ simple predicate
   ● complete subject Ⓓ complete predicate
3. We divided the money between us.
   Ⓐ simple subject ● simple predicate
   Ⓒ complete subject Ⓓ complete predicate
4. I bought this bracelet for my aunt.
   Ⓐ simple subject ● simple predicate
   Ⓒ complete subject Ⓓ complete predicate
5. Dick and his dog ran down to the beach.
   Ⓐ simple subject Ⓑ simple predicate
   ● complete subject Ⓓ complete predicate
6. My sister Katie collects stamps.
   ● simple subject Ⓑ simple predicate
   Ⓒ complete subject Ⓓ complete predicate
7. Can you call me tomorrow?
   Ⓐ simple subject ● simple predicate
   Ⓒ complete subject Ⓓ complete predicate
8. Nitasha is swimming in the lake.
   Ⓐ simple subject Ⓑ simple predicate
   Ⓒ complete subject ● complete predicate

© Mark Twain Media, Inc., Publishers 57

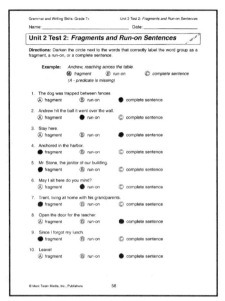

Grammar and Writing Skills: Grade 7+ Unit 2 Test 2: *Fragments and Run-on Sentences*

Name: ______________________ Date: ____________

Unit 2 Test 2: *Fragments and Run-on Sentences*

Directions: Darken the circle next to the words that correctly label the word group as a fragment, a run-on, or a complete sentence.

Example: *Andrew, reaching across the table.*
● fragment (B) run-on (C) complete sentence
(A - predicate is missing)

1. The dog was trapped between fences.
(A) fragment (B) run-on ● complete sentence
2. Andrew hit the ball it went over the wall.
(A) fragment ● run-on (C) complete sentence
3. Stay here.
(A) fragment (B) run-on ● complete sentence
4. Anchored in the harbor.
● fragment (B) run-on (C) complete sentence
5. Mr. Stone, the janitor of our building.
● fragment (B) run-on (C) complete sentence
6. May I sit here do you mind?
(A) fragment ● run-on (C) complete sentence
7. Trent, living at home with his grandparents.
● fragment (B) run-on (C) complete sentence
8. Open the door for the teacher.
(A) fragment (B) run-on ● complete sentence
9. Since I forgot my lunch.
● fragment (B) run-on (C) complete sentence
10. Leave!
(A) fragment (B) run-on ● complete sentence

© Mark Twain Media, Inc., Publishers 58

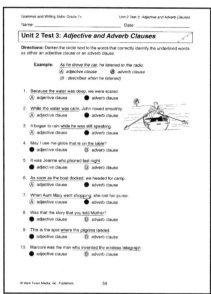

Grammar and Writing Skills: Grade 7+ Unit 2 Test 3: *Adjective and Adverb Clauses*

Name: ______________________ Date: ____________

Unit 2 Test 3: *Adjective and Adverb Clauses*

Directions: Darken the circle next to the words that correctly identify the underlined words as either an adjective clause or an adverb clause.

Example: *As he drove the car, he listened to the radio.*
(A) adjective clause ● adverb clause
(B - describes when he listened)

1. Because the water was deep, we were scared.
(A) adjective clause ● adverb clause
2. While the water was calm, John rowed smoothly.
(A) adjective clause ● adverb clause
3. It began to rain while he was still speaking.
(A) adjective clause ● adverb clause
4. May I use the globe that is on the table?
● adjective clause (B) adverb clause
5. It was Jeanne who phoned last night.
● adjective clause (B) adverb clause
6. As soon as the boat docked, we headed for camp.
(A) adjective clause ● adverb clause
7. When Aunt Mary went shopping, she lost her purse.
(A) adjective clause ● adverb clause
8. Was that the story that you told Mother?
● adjective clause (B) adverb clause
9. This is the spot where the pilgrims landed.
● adjective clause (B) adverb clause
10. Marconi was the man who invented the wireless telegraph.
● adjective clause (B) adverb clause

© Mark Twain Media, Inc., Publishers 59

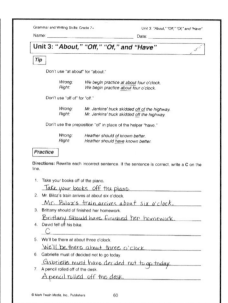

Grammar and Writing Skills: Grade 7+ Unit 3: *"About," "Off," "Of," and "Have"*

Name: ______________________ Date: ____________

Unit 3: "*About,*" "*Off,*" "*Of,*" and "*Have*"

Tip

Don't use "at about" for "about."

Wrong: We begin practice at about four o'clock.
Right: We begin practice about four o'clock.

Don't use "off of" for "off."

Wrong: Mr. Jenkins' truck skidded off of the highway.
Right: Mr. Jenkins' truck skidded off the highway.

Don't use the preposition "of" in place of the helper "have."

Wrong: Heather should of known better.
Right: Heather should have known better.

Practice

Directions: Rewrite each incorrect sentence. If the sentence is correct, write a **C** on the line.

1. Take your books off of the piano.
Take your books off the piano.
2. Mr. Biloz's train arrives at about six o'clock.
Mr. Biloz's train arrives about six o'clock.
3. Brittany should of finished her homework.
Brittany should have finished her homework.
4. David fell off his bike.
C
5. We'll be there at about three o'clock.
We'll be there about three o'clock.
6. Gabrielle must of decided not to go today.
Gabrielle must have decided not to go today.
7. A pencil rolled off of the desk.
A pencil rolled off the desk.

© Mark Twain Media, Inc., Publishers 60

Grammar and Writing Skills: Grade 7+ Unit 3: *"Beside" & "Besides"; "Between" & "Among"; "In & "Into"*

Name: ______________________ Date: ____________

Unit 3: "*Beside*" and "*Besides*"; "*Between*" and "*Among*"; and "*In*" and "*Into*"

Tip

"Beside" means "next to;" "besides" means "in addition to."

Tim is standing beside the pool.
Who is leaving besides us?

"Between" is used when its object refers to two things.
"Among" is used when its object refers to more than two.

The decision is between you and me.
The decision is among all the class members.

"In" means "within;" "into" means "from without to within."

What is in that box?
Ciara dropped the worm into the box.

Practice

Directions: Write the correct form of the word pair in parentheses in the sentence.

Example: *Place your chair beside mine, Andrea. (beside, besides)*

1. We four people must keep the secret __among__ ourselves. (between, among)
2. Put the burgers __into__ the pan. (in, into)
3. What are we having for dinner __besides__ sweet corn? (beside, besides)
4. Craig, you need to sit __between__ Cori and Brook. (between, among)
5. What do you have __in__ that trunk? (in, into)
6. Leave the gift __beside__ the porch steps. (beside, besides)
7. Please pour the oil __into__ a different container. (in, into)
8. You are __among__ my best friends. (between, among)

© Mark Twain Media, Inc., Publishers 61

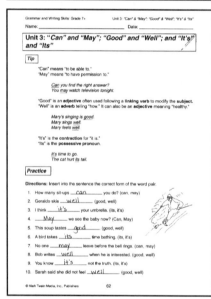

Grammar and Writing Skills: Grade 7+ Unit 3: *"Can" & "May"; "Good" & "Well"; "It's" & "Its"*

Name: ______________________ Date: ____________

Unit 3: "*Can*" and "*May*"; "*Good*" and "*Well*"; and "*It's*" and "*Its*"

Tip

"Can" means "to be able to."
"May" means "to have permission to."

Can you find the right answer?
You may watch television tonight.

"Good" is an **adjective** often used following a **linking verb** to modify the **subject.**
"Well" is an **adverb** telling "how." It can also be an **adjective** meaning "healthy."

Mary's singing is good.
Mary sings well.
Mary feels well.

"It's" is the **contraction** for "it is."
"Its" is the **possessive pronoun**.

It's time to go.
The cat hurt its tail.

Practice

Directions: Insert into the sentence the correct form of the word pair.

1. How many sit-ups __can__ you do? (can, may)
2. Geraldo skis __well__ (good, well)
3. I think __it's__ your umbrella. (its, it's)
4. __May__ we see the baby now? (Can, May)
5. This soup tastes __good__ (good, well)
6. A bird takes __its__ time bathing. (its, it's)
7. No one __may__ leave before the bell rings. (can, may)
8. Bob writes __well__ when he is interested. (good, well)
9. You know __it's__ not the truth. (its, it's)
10. Sarah said she did not feel __well__. (good, well)

© Mark Twain Media, Inc., Publishers 62

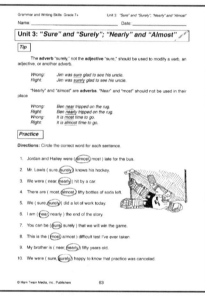

Grammar and Writing Skills: Grade 7+ Unit 3: *"Sure" and "Surely"; "Nearly" and "Almost"*

Name: ______________________ Date: ____________

Unit 3: "*Sure*" and "*Surely*"; "*Nearly*" and "*Almost*"

Tip

The **adverb** "surely," not the **adjective** "sure," should be used to modify a verb, an adjective, or another adverb.

Wrong: Jim was sure glad to see his uncle.
Right: Jim was surely glad to see his uncle.

"Nearly" and "almost" are **adverbs**. "Near" and "most" should not be used in their place

Wrong: Ben near tripped on the rug.
Right: Ben nearly tripped on the rug.
Wrong: It is most time to go.
Right: It is almost time to go.

Practice

Directions: Circle the correct word for each sentence.

1. Jordan and Hailey were (**almost**, most) late for the bus.
2. Mr. Lewis (sure, **surely**) knows his hockey.
3. We were (near, **nearly**) hit by a car.
4. There are (most, **almost**) fifty bottles of soda left.
5. We (sure, **surely**) did a lot of work today.
6. I am (**near**, nearly) the end of the story.
7. You can be (**sure**, surely) that we will win the game.
8. This is the (**most**, almost) difficult test I've ever taken.
9. My brother is (near, **nearly**) fifty years old.
10. We were (sure, **surely**) happy to know that practice was canceled.

© Mark Twain Media, Inc., Publishers 63

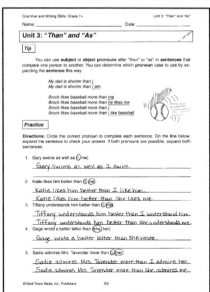

Grammar and Writing Skills: Grade 7+ Unit 3: *"Than" and "As"*

Name: ______________________ Date: ____________

Unit 3: "*Than*" and "*As*"

Tip

You can use **subject** or **object pronouns** after "than" or "as" in **sentences** that compare one person to another. You can determine which **pronoun** case to use by expanding the **sentence** this way:

My dad is shorter than I.
My dad is shorter than I am.

Brock likes baseball more than me.
Brock likes baseball more than he likes me.
Brock likes baseball more than I.
Brock likes baseball more than I like baseball.

Practice

Directions: Circle the correct pronoun to complete each sentence. On the line below, expand the sentence to check your answer. If both pronouns are possible, expand both sentences.

1. Gary swims as well as (**I**, me)
Gary swims as well as I swim.
2. Katie likes him better than (**I**, **me**).
Katie likes him better than I like him.
Katie likes him better than she likes me.
3. Tiffany understands him better than (**I**, **me**).
Tiffany understands him better than I understand him.
Tiffany understands him better than she understands me.
4. Gage wrote a better letter than (**she**, her).
Gage wrote a better letter than she wrote.
5. Sadie admires Mrs. Tavender more than (**I**, **me**)
Sadie admires Mrs. Tavender more than I admire her.
Sadie admires Mrs. Tavender more than she admires me.

© Mark Twain Media, Inc., Publishers 64

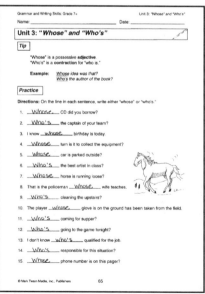

Grammar and Writing Skills: Grade 7+ Unit 3: *"Whose" and "Who's"*

Name: ______________________ Date: ____________

Unit 3: "*Whose*" and "*Who's*"

Tip

"Whose" is a possessive **adjective**.
"Who's" is a **contraction** for "who is."

Example: *Whose idea was that?*
Who's the author of the book?

Practice

Directions: On the line in each sentence, write either "whose" or "who's."

1. __Whose__ CD did you borrow?
2. __Who's__ the captain of your team?
3. I know __whose__ birthday is today.
4. __Whose__ turn is it to collect the equipment?
5. __Whose__ car is parked outside?
6. __Who's__ the best artist in class?
7. __Whose__ horse is running loose?
8. That is the policeman __whose__ wife teaches.
9. __Who's__ cleaning the upstairs?
10. The player __whose__ glove is on the ground has been taken from the field.
11. __Who's__ coming for supper?
12. __Who's__ going to the game tonight?
13. I don't know __who's__ qualified for the job.
14. __Who's__ responsible for this situation?
15. __Whose__ phone number is on this pager?

© Mark Twain Media, Inc., Publishers 65

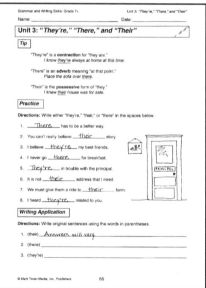

Grammar and Writing Skills: Grade 7+ Unit 3: *"They're," "There," and "Their"*

Name: ______________________ Date: ____________

Unit 3: "*They're,*" "*There,*" and "*Their*"

Tip

"They're" is a **contraction** for "they are."
I know they're always at home at this time.

"There" is an **adverb** meaning "at that point."
Place the sofa over there.

"Their" is the **possessive** form of "they."
I knew their house was for sale.

Practice

Directions: Write either "they're," "their," or "there" in the spaces below.

1. __There__ has to be a better way.
2. You can't really believe __their__ story.
3. I believe __they're__ my best friends.
4. I never go __there__ for breakfast.
5. __They're__ in trouble with the principal.
6. It is not __their__ address that I need.
7. We must give them a ride to __their__ farm.
8. I heard __they're__ related to you.

Writing Application

Directions: Write original sentences using the words in parentheses.

1. (their) Answers will vary.
2. (there) ______________________
3. (they're) ______________________

© Mark Twain Media, Inc., Publishers 66

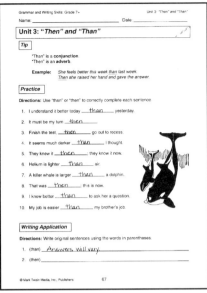

Unit 3: "Then" and "Than"

Tip

"Than" is a **conjunction**.
"Then" is an **adverb**.

Example: She feels better this week than last week.
Then she raised her hand and gave the answer.

Practice

Directions: Use "than" or "then" to correctly complete each sentence.

1. I understand it better today __than__ yesterday.
2. It must be my turn __then__.
3. Finish the test __then__ go out to recess.
4. It seems much darker __than__ I thought.
5. They knew it __then__; they know it now.
6. Helium is lighter __than__ air.
7. A killer whale is larger __than__ a dolphin.
8. That was __then__; this is now.
9. I knew better __than__ to ask her a question.
10. My job is easier __than__ my brother's job.

Writing Application

Directions: Write original sentences using the words in parentheses.

1. (than) __Answers will vary.__
2. (then) _____

67

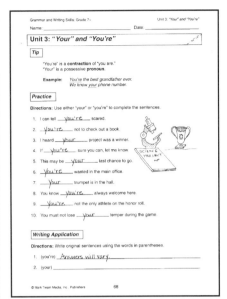

Unit 3: "Your" and "You're"

Tip

"You're" is a **contraction** of "you are."
"Your" is a possessive **pronoun**.

Example: You're the best grandfather ever.
We know your phone number.

Practice

Directions: Use either "your" or "you're" to complete the sentences.

1. I can tell __you're__ scared.
2. __You're__ not to check out a book.
3. I heard __your__ project was a winner.
4. If __you're__ sure you can, let me know.
5. This may be __your__ last chance to go.
6. __You're__ wanted in the main office.
7. __Your__ trumpet is in the hall.
8. You know __you're__ always welcome here.
9. __You're__ not the only athlete on the honor roll.
10. You must not lose __your__ temper during the game.

Writing Application

Directions: Write original sentences using the words in parentheses.

1. (you're) __Answers will vary.__
2. (your) _____

68

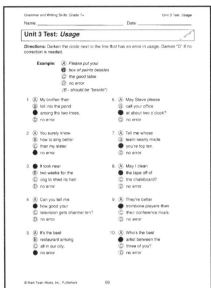

Unit 3 Test: Usage

Directions: Darken the circle next to the line that has an error in usage. Darken "D" if no correction is needed.

Example: Ⓐ Please put your
Ⓑ box of paints besides
Ⓒ the good table
Ⓓ no error
(B - should be "beside")

1. Ⓐ My brother then
   Ⓑ fell into the pond
   ● among the two trees.
   Ⓓ no error

2. Ⓐ You surely know
   Ⓑ how to sing better
   Ⓒ than my sister.
   ● no error

3. ● It took near
   Ⓑ two weeks for the
   Ⓒ dog to shed its hair.
   Ⓓ no error

4. Ⓐ Can you tell me
   ● how good your
   Ⓒ television gets channel ten?
   Ⓓ no error

5. ● It's the best
   Ⓑ restaurant among
   Ⓒ all in our city.
   Ⓓ no error

6. Ⓐ May Steve please
   Ⓑ call your office
   ● at about two o'clock?
   Ⓓ no error

7. Ⓐ Tell me whose
   ● team nearly made
   Ⓒ you're top ten.
   Ⓓ no error

8. ● May I clean
   Ⓑ the tape off of
   Ⓒ the chalkboard?
   Ⓓ no error

9. Ⓐ They're better
   ● trombone players then
   Ⓒ their conference rivals.
   Ⓓ no error

10. Ⓐ Who's the best
    ● artist between the
    Ⓒ three of you?
    Ⓓ no error

69

Unit 3 Test: Usage (Continued)

11. ● You can enter
    Ⓑ the poster contest
    Ⓒ if you're ready.
    Ⓓ no error

12. Ⓐ I know well
    ● that there the
    Ⓒ students to blame
    Ⓓ no error

13. Ⓐ Only one person
    ● besides me was
    Ⓒ invited into the Honors Club.
    Ⓓ no error

14. ● Beside Sheila,
    Ⓑ there were two other
    Ⓒ girls in the play.
    Ⓓ no error

15. ● She should of
    Ⓑ gone home
    Ⓒ right after school.
    Ⓓ no error

16. Ⓐ I am sure that
    Ⓑ your bread tastes
    Ⓒ better than mine.
    ● no error

17. Jason near walked
    Ⓑ into the tree
    Ⓒ before he stopped.
    Ⓓ no error

18. Ⓐ Is Kyra as
    Ⓑ short as
    ● me?
    Ⓓ no error

19. Ⓐ Jamal can run
    Ⓑ faster than
    Ⓒ I.
    ● no error

20. Ⓐ He is coming
    Ⓑ to dinner
    ● at about six o'clock.
    Ⓓ no error

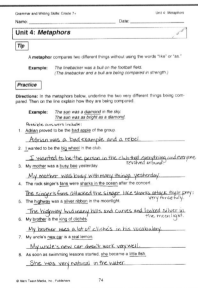

70

Unit 4: Prefixes

Tip

A **prefix** is placed at the beginning of a word to change the meaning. Some common **prefixes** are:

ad - to	**de** - down	**post** - after
pre - before	**sub** - under	**trans** - across
anti - against	**ex** - out	**in** - not
mis - wrong	**non** - not	**super** - above

Writing Application

Directions: Add one of the prefixes above to each word in parentheses. Then write an original sentence using the word correctly.

Example: (spell) misspell   Don't misspell another word.

1. (sonic) __supersonic__
   __Sentences will vary.__
2. (conscious) __subconscious__
3. (mature) __immature__
4. (continental) __transcontinental__
5. (violent) __nonviolent__
6. (visible) __invisible__
7. (absorbent) __nonabsorbent__

71

Unit 4: Suffixes

Tip

A **suffix** is placed at the end of a word. Some common suffixes are:

able - can be	**less** - without	**er** - one who does
ness - quality of	**ish** - like, somewhat	**ful** - full of

Writing Application

Directions: Add one of the suffixes above to each word in parentheses. Then write an original sentence using the word correctly.

Example: (like) likable   She is a likable young lady.
Possible answers include:
1. (help) __helpless, helpful, helper__
   __Sentences will vary.__
2. (child) __childish__
3. (gentle) __gentleness__
4. (read) __readable, reader__
5. (hope) __hopeless, hopeful, hoper__
6. (play) __playable, playful, player__
7. (green) __greenish__
8. (color) __colorless, colorful, colorer__
9. (fool) __foolish__
10. (kind) __kindness__

72

Unit 4: Metaphors

Tip

A **metaphor** compares two different things without using the words "like" or "as."

Example: The linebacker was a bull on the football field.
(The linebacker and a bull are being compared in strength.)

Practice

Directions: In the metaphors below, underline the two very different things being compared. Then on the line explain how they are being compared.

Example: The sun was a diamond in the sky.
The sun was as bright as a diamond.

Possible answers include:
1. Adrian proved to be the bad apple of the group.
   __Adrian was a bad example and a rebel.__
2. I wanted to be the big wheel in the club.
   __I wanted to be the person in the club that everything and everyone revolved around.__
3. My mother was a busy bee yesterday.
   __My mother was busy with many things yesterday.__
4. The rock singer's fans were sharks in the ocean after the concert.
   __The singer's fans attacked the singer like sharks attack their prey; very forcefully.__
5. The highway was a silver ribbon in the moonlight.
   __The highway had many hills and curves and looked silver in the moonlight.__
6. My brother is the king of clichés.
   __My brother uses a lot of clichés in his vocabulary.__
7. My uncle's new car is a real lemon.
   __My uncle's new car doesn't work very well.__
8. As soon as swimming lessons started, she became a little fish.
   __She was very natural in the water.__

74

Unit 4: Similes

Tip

A **simile** compares two very different things using the words "like" or "as."

Example: The volunteer worker was like an angel to us.
(both are surprising helpers)

Practice

Directions: Underline the objects being compared in each sentence and circle the "like" or "as." On the line explain how the objects are being compared.

Possible answers include:
1. The wet carpet was (as) soft as a sponge.
   __The wet carpet was very soft and squishy.__
2. Dee was so embarrassed, she looked (like) a beet.
   __Dee was so embarrassed that her face turned bright red.__
3. Bob was very scared, his legs were (like) gelatin.
   __Bob's legs were unstable and very wobbly and weak.__
4. From the air, the houses looked (like) shoe boxes fitted together.
   __The houses were the same size and shape.__
5. The sprinter was (like) the wind.
   __The sprinter was very fast and graceful.__
6. My anger was (as) explosive as a grenade.
   __I get angry very quickly and violently.__
7. Mrs. Charlson's voice was (like) a foghorn.
   __Mrs. Charlson's voice had a monotone, annoying sound.__

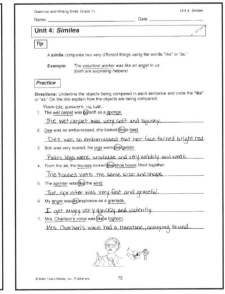

75

Unit 4: Double Negatives

Tip

Do not use more than one **negative** word in the same sentence. Do not use a **negative** in a sentence with "hardly," "barely," or "scarcely." Also, the words "no," "none," "never," "nobody," "nowhere," and "nothing" are negative along with the word "not."

Wrong: I don't have no money.
Right: I don't have any money.
Right: I do have no money.

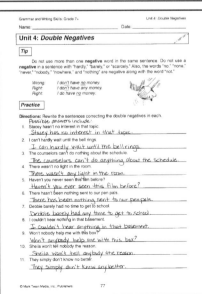

Practice

Directions: Rewrite the sentences correcting the double negatives in each.
Possible answers include:
1. Stacey hasn't no interest in that topic.
   __Stacey has no interest in that topic.__
2. I can't hardly wait until the bell rings.
   __I can hardly wait until the bell rings.__
3. The counselors can't do nothing about the schedule.
   __The counselors can't do anything about the schedule.__
4. There wasn't no light in the room.
   __There wasn't any light in the room.__
5. Haven't you never seen this film before?
   __Haven't you ever seen this film before?__
6. There hasn't been nothing sent to our pen pals.
   __There has been nothing sent to our pen pals.__
7. Debbie barely had no time to get to school.
   __Debbie barely had any time to get to school.__
8. I couldn't hear nothing in that basement.
   __I couldn't hear anything in that basement.__
9. Won't nobody help me with this box?
   __Won't anybody help me with this box?__
10. Sheila won't tell nobody the reason.
    __Sheila won't tell anybody the reason.__
11. They simply don't know no better.
    __They simply don't know any better.__

77

121

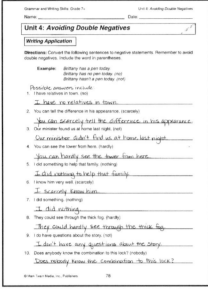

Unit 4: Avoiding Double Negatives

Writing Application

Directions: Convert the following sentences to negative statements. Remember to avoid double negatives. Include the word in parentheses.

Example: Brittany has a pen today.
Brittany has no pen today. (no)
Brittany hasn't a pen today. (not)

Possible answers include:
1. I have relatives in town. (no)
   I have no relatives in town.
2. You can tell the difference in his appearance. (scarcely)
   You can scarcely tell the difference in his appearance.
3. Our minister found us at home last night. (not)
   Our minister didn't find us at home last night.
4. You can see the tower from here. (hardly)
   You can hardly see the tower from here.
5. I did something to help that family. (nothing)
   I did nothing to help that family.
6. I know him very well. (scarcely)
   I scarcely know him.
7. I did something. (nothing)
   I did nothing.
8. They could see through the thick fog. (hardly)
   They could hardly see through the thick fog.
9. I do have questions about the story. (hardly)
   I don't have any questions about the story.
10. Does anybody know the combination to this lock? (nobody)
    Does nobody know the combination to this lock?

© Mark Twain Media, Inc., Publishers   78

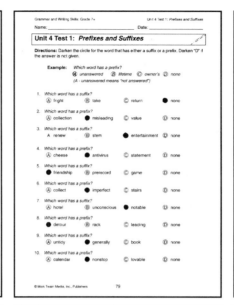

Unit 4 Test 1: Prefixes and Suffixes

Directions: Darken the circle for the word that has either a suffix or a prefix. Darken "D" if the answer is not given.

Example: Which word has a prefix?
(A) unanswered (B) lifetime (C) owner's (D) none
(A - unanswered means 'not answered')

1. Which word has a suffix?
   (A) fright (B) take (C) return ● none
2. Which word has a prefix?
   (A) collection ● misleading (C) value (D) none
3. Which word has a suffix?
   A renew (B) stem ● entertainment (D) none
4. Which word has a prefix?
   (A) cheese ● antivirus (C) statement (D) none
5. Which word has a suffix?
   ● friendship (B) prerecord (C) game (D) none
6. Which word has a prefix?
   (A) collect ● imperfect (C) stairs (D) none
7. Which word has a suffix?
   (A) hotel (B) unconscious ● notable (D) none
8. Which word has a prefix?
   ● detour (B) rack (C) leading (D) none
9. Which word has a suffix?
   (A) unticy ● generally (C) book (D) none
10. Which word has a prefix?
    (A) calendar ● nonstop (C) lovable (D) none

© Mark Twain Media, Inc., Publishers   79

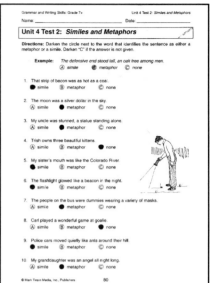

Unit 4 Test 2: Similes and Metaphors

Directions: Darken the circle next to the word that identifies the sentence as either a metaphor or a simile. Darken "C" if the answer is not given.

Example: The defensive end stood tall, an oak tree among men.
(A) simile ● metaphor (C) none

1. That strip of bacon was as hot as a coal.
   ● simile (B) metaphor (C) none
2. The moon was a silver dollar in the sky.
   (A) simile ● metaphor (C) none
3. My uncle was stunned, a statue standing alone.
   (A) simile ● metaphor (C) none
4. Trish owns three beautiful kittens.
   (A) simile (B) metaphor ● none
5. My sister's mouth was like the Colorado River.
   ● simile (B) metaphor (C) none
6. The flashlight glowed like a beacon in the night.
   ● simile (B) metaphor (C) none
7. The people on the bus were dummies wearing a variety of masks.
   (A) simile ● metaphor (C) none
8. Carl played a wonderful game at goalie.
   (A) simile (B) metaphor ● none
9. Police cars moved quietly like ants around their hill.
   ● simile (B) metaphor (C) none
10. My granddaughter was an angel all night long.
    (A) simile ● metaphor (C) none

© Mark Twain Media, Inc., Publishers   80

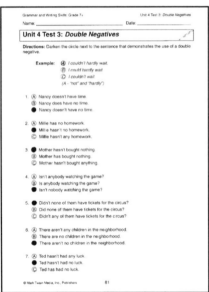

Unit 4 Test 3: Double Negatives

Directions: Darken the circle next to the sentence that demonstrates the use of a double negative.

Example: (A) I couldn't hardly wait.
(B) I could hardly wait.
(C) I couldn't wait.
(A - 'not' and 'hardly')

1. (A) Nancy doesn't have time.
   (B) Nancy does have no time.
   ● Nancy doesn't have no time.
2. (A) Millie has no homework.
   ● Millie hasn't no homework.
   (C) Millie hasn't any homework.
3. ● Mother hasn't bought nothing.
   (B) Mother has bought something.
   (C) Mother hasn't bought anything.
4. (A) Isn't anybody watching the game?
   (B) Is anybody watching the game?
   ● Isn't nobody watching the game?
5. ● Didn't none of them have tickets for the circus?
   (B) Did none of them have tickets for the circus?
   (C) Didn't any of them have tickets for the circus?
6. (A) There aren't any children in the neighborhood.
   (B) There are no children in the neighborhood.
   ● There aren't no children in the neighborhood.
7. (A) Ted hasn't had any luck.
   ● Ted hasn't had no luck.
   (C) Ted has no luck.

© Mark Twain Media, Inc., Publishers   81

Unit 5: Capitalization Practice

Practice

Directions: Rewrite each sentence, making corrections in capitalization.

1. I am collecting for easter seals this year.
   I am collecting for Easter Seals this year.
2. We camped at duncan park in indiana.
   We camped at Duncan Park in Indiana.
3. Steve borrowed the adventures of tom sawyer from the library.
   Steve borrowed The Adventures of Tom Sawyer from the library.
4. The ohio river empties into the mississippi river.
   The Ohio River empties into the Mississippi River.
5. The constitution replaced the articles of confederation.
   The Constitution replaced the Articles of Confederation.
6. We saw mount rainier in washington.
   We saw Mount Rainier in Washington.
7. I attended douglas high school on fulton avenue.
   I attended Douglas High School on Fulton Avenue.
8. We have no school on columbus day and veterans' day.
   We have no school on Columbus Day and Veterans' Day.
9. They saw the statue of liberty on liberty island in new york.
   They saw the Statue of Liberty on Liberty Island in New York.
10. I had to read call of the wild for a report.
    I had to read Call of the Wild for a report.

© Mark Twain Media, Inc., Publishers   83

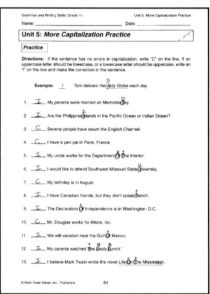

Unit 5: More Capitalization Practice

Practice

Directions: If the sentence has no errors in capitalization, write "C" on the line. If an uppercase letter should be lowercase, or a lowercase letter should be uppercase, write an "I" on the line and make the correction in the sentence.

Example: I   Tom delivers the daily Globe each day. (D)

1. I   My parents were married on Memorial Day.
2. I   Are the Philippine Islands in the Pacific Ocean or Indian Ocean?
3. C   Several people have swum the English Channel.
4. C   I have a pen pal in Paris, France.
5. I   My uncle works for the Department of the Interior.
6. I   I would like to attend Southwest Missouri State University.
7. I   My birthday is in August.
8. I   I have Canadian friends, but they don't speak French.
9. I   The Declaration of Independence is in Washington, D.C.
10. C   Mr. Douglas works for Atkins, Inc.
11. I   We will vacation near the Gulf of Mexico.
12. I   My parents watched the Brady Bunch.
13. I   I believe Mark Twain wrote the novel Life On the Mississippi.

© Mark Twain Media, Inc., Publishers   84

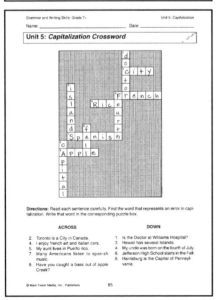

Unit 5: Capitalization Crossword

Crossword puzzle answers:
city, French, Rico, island, Spanish, Apple, capital

Directions: Read each sentence carefully. Find the word that represents an error in capitalization. Write that word in the corresponding puzzle box.

ACROSS
2. Toronto is a City in Canada.
4. I enjoy french art and Italian cars.
5. My aunt lives in Puerto rico.
7. Many Americans listen to spanish music.
8. Have you caught a bass out of apple Creek?

DOWN
1. Is the Doctor at Williams Hospital?
3. Hawaii has several Islands.
4. My uncle was born on the fourth of July.
6. Jefferson High School starts in the Fall.
8. Harrisburg is the Capital of Pennsylvania.

© Mark Twain Media, Inc., Publishers   85

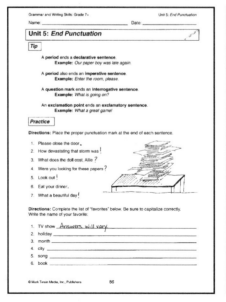

Unit 5: End Punctuation

Tip

A period ends a **declarative sentence.**
Example: Our paper boy was late again.

A period also ends an **imperative sentence.**
Example: Enter the room, please.

A question mark ends an **interrogative sentence.**
Example: What is going on?

An exclamation point ends an **exclamatory sentence.**
Example: What a great game!

Practice

Directions: Place the proper punctuation mark at the end of each sentence.

1. Please close the door.
2. How devastating that storm was !
3. What does the doll cost, Allie ?
4. Were you looking for these papers ?
5. Look out !
6. Eat your dinner.
7. What a beautiful day !

Directions: Complete the list of "favorites" below. Be sure to capitalize correctly. Write the name of your favorite:

1. TV show   Answers will vary
2. holiday _____
3. month _____
4. city _____
5. song _____
6. book _____

© Mark Twain Media, Inc., Publishers   86

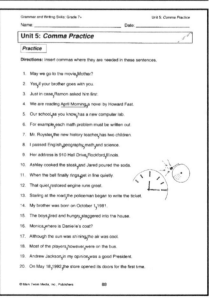

Unit 5: Comma Practice

Practice

Directions: Insert commas where they are needed in these sentences.

1. May we go to the movie, Mother?
2. Yes, if your brother goes with you.
3. Just in case, Ramon asked him first.
4. We are reading April Morning, a novel by Howard Fast.
5. Our school, as you know, has a new computer lab.
6. For example, each math problem must be written out.
7. Mr. Royster, the new history teacher, has two children.
8. I passed English, geography, math, and science.
9. Her address is 910 Hall Drive, Rockford, Illinois.
10. Ashley cooked the steak, and Jared poured the soda.
11. When the bell finally rings, get in line quietly.
12. That quiet, restored engine runs great.
13. Staring at the road, the policeman began to write the ticket.
14. My brother was born on October 1, 1981.
15. The boys, tired and hungry, staggered into the house.
16. Monica, where is Danielle's coat?
17. Although the sun was shining, the air was cool.
18. Most of the players, however, were on the bus.
19. Andrew Jackson, in my opinion, was a good President.
20. On May 18, 1992, the store opened its doors for the first time.

© Mark Twain Media, Inc., Publishers   88

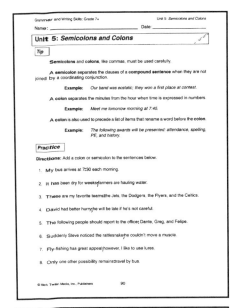

Unit 5: Semicolons and Colons

Tip

Semicolons and colons, like commas, must be used carefully.

A **semicolon** separates the clauses of a **compound sentence** when they are not joined by a coordinating conjunction.

Example: *Our band was ecstatic; they won first place at contest.*

A **colon** separates the minutes from the hour when time is expressed in numbers.

Example: *Meet me tomorrow morning at 7:45.*

A **colon** is also used to precede a list of items that rename a word before the **colon**.

Example: *The following awards will be presented: attendance, spelling, PE, and history.*

Practice

Directions: Add a colon or semicolon to the sentences below.

1. My bus arrives at 7:30 each morning.
2. It has been dry for weeks; farmers are hauling water.
3. These are my favorite teams: the Jets, the Dodgers, the Flyers, and the Celtics.
4. David had better hurry; he will be late if he's not careful.
5. The following people should report to the office: Dante, Greg, and Felipe.
6. Suddenly Steve noticed the rattlesnake; he couldn't move a muscle.
7. Fly-fishing has great appeal; however, I like to use lures.
8. Only one other possibility remains: travel by bus.

90

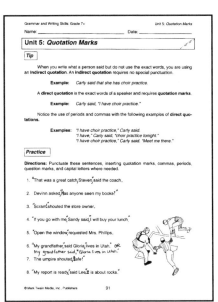

Unit 5: Quotation Marks

Tip

When you write what a person said but do not use the exact words, you are using an **indirect quotation**. An **indirect quotation** requires no special punctuation.

Example: *Carly said that she has choir practice.*

A **direct quotation** is the exact words of a speaker and requires **quotation marks**.

Example: *Carly said, "I have choir practice."*

Notice the use of periods and commas with the following examples of **direct quotations**.

Examples: *"I have choir practice," Carly said.*
"I have," Carly said, "choir practice tonight."
"I have choir practice," Carly said. "Meet me there."

Practice

Directions: Punctuate these sentences, inserting quotation marks, commas, periods, question marks, and capital letters where needed.

1. "That was a great catch, Steven," said the coach.
2. Devinn asked, "Has anyone seen my books?"
3. "Scram!" shouted the store owner.
4. "If you go with me, Sandy said, "I will buy your lunch."
5. "Open the window," requested Mrs. Phillips.
6. "My grandfather," said Gloria, "lives in Utah." OR "My grandfather said," Gloria lives in Utah."
7. The umpire shouted, "Safe!"
8. "My report is ready," said Lee, "it is about rocks."

91

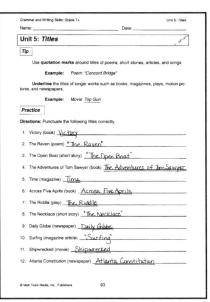

Unit 5: Titles

Tip

Use **quotation marks** around titles of poems, short stories, articles, and songs.

Example: *Poem: "Concord Bridge"*

Underline the titles of longer works such as books, magazines, plays, motion pictures, and newspapers.

Example: *Movie: Top Gun*

Practice

Directions: Punctuate the following titles correctly.

1. Victory (book) Victory
2. The Raven (poem) "The Raven"
3. The Open Boat (short story) "The Open Boat"
4. The Adventures of Tom Sawyer (book) The Adventures of Tom Sawyer
5. Time (magazine) Time
6. Across Five Aprils (book) Across Five Aprils
7. The Riddle (play) The Riddle
8. The Necklace (short story) "The Necklace"
9. Daily Globe (newspaper) Daily Globe
10. Surfing (magazine article) "Surfing"
11. Shipwrecked (movie) Shipwrecked
12. Atlanta Constitution (newspaper) Atlanta Constitution

93

Unit 5: Writing Titles

Writing Application

Directions: Write a title for each of the following. Remember to punctuate and capitalize correctly.

1. a book Answers will vary.
2. a short poem
3. a magazine
4. a play
5. a short story
6. a song
7. a newspaper
8. a magazine

Directions: Rewrite the sentences below using correct punctuation.

1. Have you ever read the book A Bell For Adano?
   Have you ever read the book A Bell For Adano?
2. I took my cousin to rent the movie Titanic.
   I took my cousin to rent the movie Titanic.
3. I enjoy singing Happy Birthday.
   I enjoy singing "Happy Birthday."
4. My uncle subscribes to the magazine The Sign.
   My uncle subscribes to the magazine The Sign.
5. Who wrote the story The Great Stone Face?
   Who wrote the story "The Great Stone Face"?

94

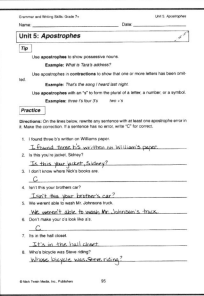

Unit 5: Apostrophes

Tip

Use **apostrophes** to show possessive nouns.

Example: *What is Tara's address?*

Use apostrophes in **contractions** to show that one or more letters has been omitted.

Example: *That's the song I heard last night.*

Use apostrophes with an "s" to make the plural of a letter, a number, or a symbol.

Examples: *three t's four 3's   two +'s*

Practice

Directions: On the lines below, rewrite each sentence with at least one apostrophe error in it. Make the correction. If a sentence has no error, write "C" for correct.

1. I found three b's written on Williams paper.
   I found three b's written on William's paper.
2. Is this you're jacket, Sidney?
   Is this your jacket, Sidney?
3. I don't know where Nick's books are.
   C
4. Isn't this your brothers car?
   Isn't this your brother's car?
5. We werent able to wash Mr. Johnsons truck.
   We weren't able to wash Mr. Johnson's truck.
6. Don't make your o's look like a's.
   C
7. Its in the hall closet.
   It's in the hall closet.
8. Who's bicycle was Steve riding?
   Whose bicycle was Steve riding?

95

Unit 5: Capitalization and Punctuation Review

Practice

Directions: Rewrite the following sentences using correct punctuation and capitalization.

Example: *color photography was developed by auguste and louis lumiere on january 3 1907.*

Color photography was developed by Auguste and Louis Lumiere on January 3, 1907.

1. in february of 1916 americans were first introduced to windshield wipers.
   In February of 1916, Americans were first introduced to windshield wipers.
2. charles lindbergh on march 14 1927 made his great nonstop solo flight across the atlantic ocean.
   Charles Lindbergh on March 14, 1927, made his great nonstop solo flight across the Atlantic Ocean.
3. on april 24 1939 german and soviet forces occupied poland, starting ww ll.
   On April 24, 1939, German and Soviet forces occupied Poland, starting WWII.
4. the great jackie robinson broke the race barrier in major league baseball on may 8 1947.
   The great Jackie Robinson broke the race barrier in Major League baseball on May 8, 1947.
5. the first artificial satellite sputnik i was launched by the soviets on october 4 1957.
   The first artificial satellite, Sputnik I, was launched by the Soviets on October 4, 1957.
6. in august of 1968 rev dr martin luther king jr was assassinated in memphis tennessee.
   In August of 1968, Rev. Dr. Martin Luther King, Jr., was assassinated in Memphis, Tennessee.

97

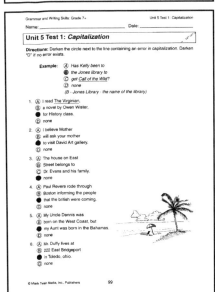

Unit 5 Test 1: Capitalization

Directions: Darken the circle next to the line containing an error in capitalization. Darken "D" if no error exists.

Example: Ⓐ Has Kelly been to
Ⓑ the Jones library to
● get *Call of the Wild*?
Ⓓ none
(B - Jones Library - the name of the library)

1. Ⓐ I read *The Virginian*,
   ● a novel by Owen Wister,
   Ⓒ for History class.
   Ⓓ none
2. Ⓐ I believe Mother
   ● will ask your mother
   Ⓒ to visit David Art gallery.
   Ⓓ none
3. Ⓐ The house on East
   Ⓑ Street belongs to
   Ⓒ Dr. Evans and his family.
   ● none
4. Ⓐ Paul Revere rode through
   Ⓑ Boston informing the people
   ● that the british were coming.
   Ⓓ none
5. Ⓐ My Uncle Dennis was
   Ⓑ born on the West Coast, but
   ● my Aunt was born in the Bahamas.
   Ⓓ none
6. Ⓐ Mr. Duffy lives at
   Ⓑ 222 East Bridgeport
   ● in Toledo, ohio.
   Ⓓ none

99

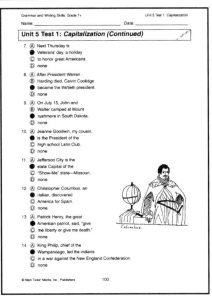

Unit 5 Test 1: Capitalization (Continued)

7. ● Next Thursday is
   Ⓑ Veterans' day, a holiday
   Ⓒ to honor great Americans.
   Ⓓ none
8. Ⓐ After President Warren
   Ⓑ Harding died, Calvin Coolidge
   ● became the thirtieth president.
   Ⓓ none
9. Ⓐ On July 15, John and
   Ⓑ Walter camped at Mount
   ● rushmore in South Dakota.
   Ⓓ none
10. Ⓐ Jeanne Goodwin, my cousin,
    Ⓑ is the President of the
    ● high school Latin Club.
    Ⓓ none
11. Ⓐ Jefferson City is the
    ● state Capital of the
    Ⓒ "Show-Me" state—Missouri.
    Ⓓ none
12. Ⓐ Christopher Columbus, an
    ● italian, discovered
    Ⓒ America for Spain.
    Ⓓ none
13. Ⓐ Patrick Henry, the great
    Ⓑ American patriot, said, "give
    ● me liberty or give me death."
    Ⓓ none
14. Ⓐ King Philip, chief of the
    ● Wampanoago, led the indians
    Ⓒ in a war against the New England Confederation.
    Ⓓ none

Columbus

100

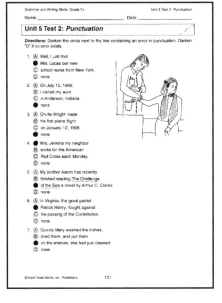

Unit 5 Test 2: Punctuation

Directions: Darken the circle next to the line containing an error in punctuation. Darken "D" if no error exists.

1. Ⓐ Well, I just met
   ● Mrs. Lucas our new
   Ⓒ school nurse from New York.
   Ⓓ none
2. Ⓐ On July 15, 1996,
   Ⓑ I visited my aunt
   Ⓒ in Anderson, Indiana.
   ● none
3. Ⓐ Orville Wright made
   Ⓑ his first plane flight
   Ⓒ on January 12, 1908.
   ● none
4. Ⓐ Mrs. Jenkins my neighbor
   Ⓑ works for the American
   Ⓒ Red Cross each Monday.
   ● none
5. Ⓐ My brother Aaron has recently
   Ⓑ finished reading The Challenge
   ● of the Sea a novel by Arthur C. Clarke.
   Ⓓ none
6. Ⓐ In Virginia, the great patriot
   Ⓑ Patrick Henry, fought against
   ● the passing of the Constitution.
   Ⓓ none
7. Ⓐ Quickly Mary washed the dishes,
   Ⓑ dried them, and put them
   ● on the shelves, she had just cleaned.
   Ⓓ none

101

Unit 5 Test 2: *Punctuation (Continued)*

8. ● Yes if Toby goes with you,
    Ⓑ you mustn't be out too
    Ⓒ late; he has a game tomorrow.
    Ⓓ none

9. Ⓐ When you finish your homework,
    Ⓑ Richard, please help me
    Ⓒ move the Smiths' piano.
    ● none

10. Ⓐ I've completed all my
    ● homework in history
    Ⓒ geography, English, and art.
    Ⓓ none

11. Ⓐ Trent, at this time of year,
    Ⓑ as you know, students visit
    ● the library to do they're research.
    Ⓓ none

12. Ⓐ Mrs. Arnold's appearance
    Ⓑ at the dance wasn't, of
    Ⓒ course, a shock to any of us.
    ● none

13. Ⓐ The following students have
    Ⓑ been awarded medals: Ann,
    ● Linda, Luanne, and Ginger
    Ⓓ none

14. Ⓐ The 7:50 train to
    ● Detroit, Michigan has
    Ⓒ been canceled, so I've heard.
    Ⓓ none.

15. Ⓐ Cora Davenport, our
    Ⓑ chemistry teacher, graduated
    Ⓒ from Texas Tech University.
    ● none

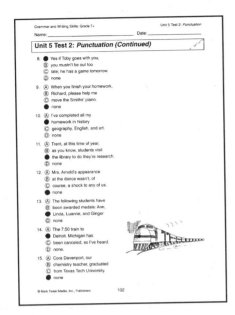